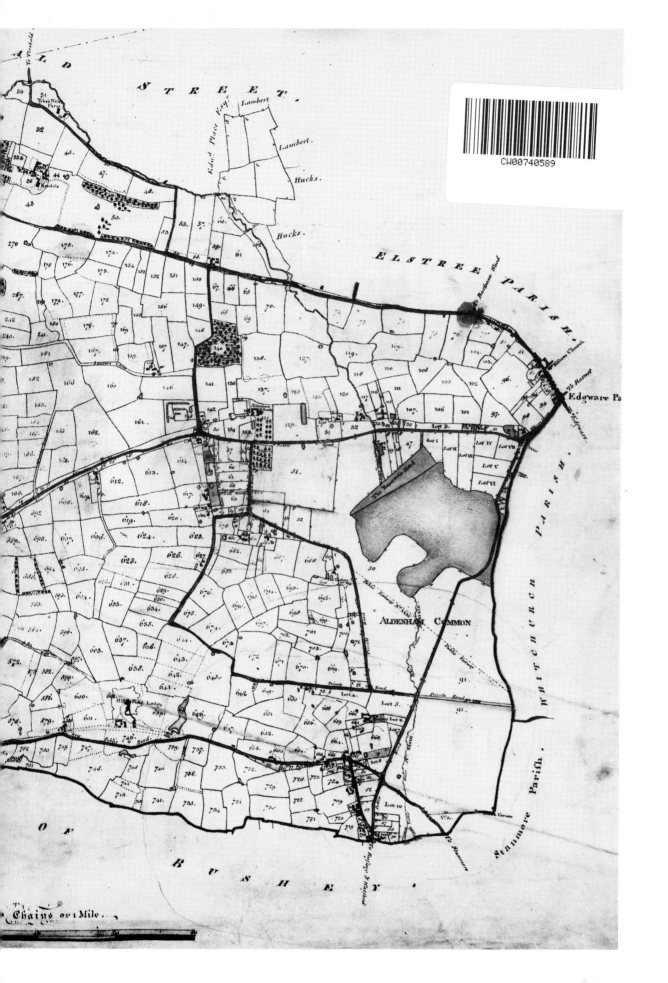

The Book of Radlett & Aldenham 1990
has been published
in a Limited Edition
of which this is

Number 251

A complete list of
subscribers is printed
at the back of the book

THE BOOK OF RADLETT & ALDENHAM

FRONT COVER: The old Red Lion at Radlett in about 1890, from a
contemporary painting now in the possession of Peter Burrell.

Aldenham Parish Church of St John the Baptist, c1800.

THE BOOK OF
RADLETT &
ALDENHAM

BY

DONALD WRATTEN

Donald Wratten

4 May 1990

BARRACUDA BOOKS LIMITED
BUCKINGHAM, ENGLAND
MCMXC

PUBLISHED BY BARRACUDA BOOKS LIMITED
BUCKINGHAM, ENGLAND

AND PRINTED BY
H.E. BODDY & CO LIMITED
BANBURY, OXON

BOUND BY
HUNTER & FOULIS LIMITED
EDINBURGH, SCOTLAND

JACKETS PRINTED BY
CHENEY & SONS LIMITED
BANBURY, OXON

LITHOGRAPHY BY
SOUTH MIDLANDS LITHOPLATES LIMITED
LUTON, ENGLAND

TYPESET BY
KEYBOARD SERVICES
LUTON, ENGLAND

ISBN 0 86023 464 9

Contents

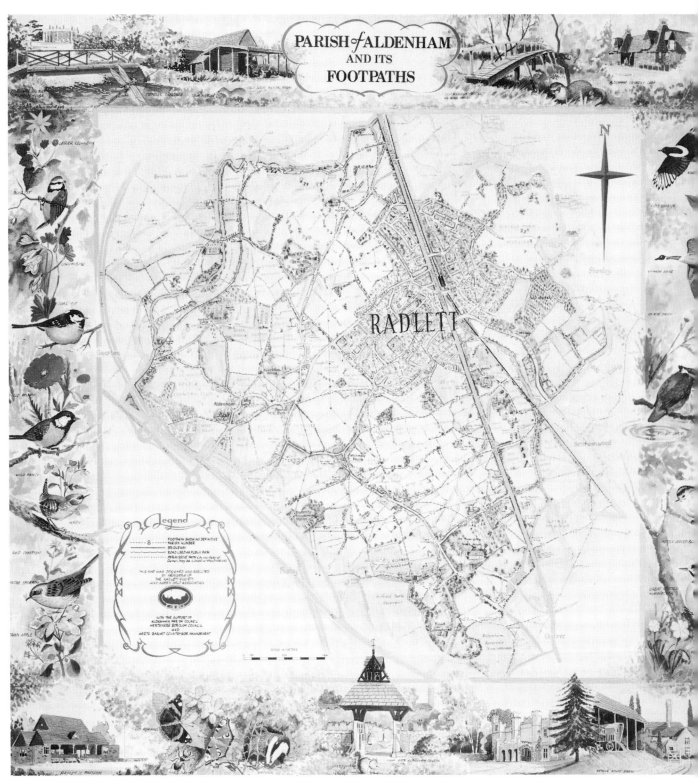

PARISH of ALDENHAM AND ITS FOOTPATHS

RADLETT

The Parish of Aldenham 1989 — drawn and coloured by Ted Barker and
Tony Jennings for the Radlett Society & Green Belt Association.

Acknowledgements

This book could not have been written without the information on the Parish of Aldenham amassed by the late Harold Knee. Harold, who lived in Radlett for 76 of his 89 years, spent his retirement researching in great depth the history of the Parish and undoubtedly, had time not run out on him, would have been the author of the present volume. Shortly before his death in 1987 he presented me with his extensive manuscript notes and these have formed the basis of much of the text. As a result I have been saved considerable time and effort in the compilation of factual information for the book, particularly in regard to material derived from the Hertfordshire Record Office, but nevertheless I should like to thank Peter Walne and his staff for the facilities and help they kindly afforded Harold Knee in the first place. Thanks also go to all the other people with whom Harold corresponded and who so willingly supplied him with much invaluable information on points of detail. Although space restrictions have prevented the use of much of this information it is being carefully preserved by the Radlett Local History Society for future reference.

My special thanks are also due to David Spain, who has helped so much with the illustrations. Although the majority of these come from original postcards and other photographs in my personal collection, or that of the Local History Society, David has freely and voluntarily used his immense skills as a professional photographer to enhance the quality for reproduction. He has also made original prints from negatives of local photographs taken by F.H. Stingemore, an enthusiastic amateur photographer who lived in Radlett between the 1920s and '50s, which had been acquired from his widow by the Hertfordshire Record Office, whose permission to use them as illustrations we gladly acknowledge. Thanks are also due to the British Library, the Royal Commission on Historic Monuments, the Public Records Office, the Verulamium Museum and the Dean and Chapter of Westminster Abbey for permission to use copyright material supplied by them.

Many local people have generously helped me with information, comment and illustrative material. Among these I must particularly acknowledge the assistance of Ronald Burnell, Tessa Carrington, Stephen Castle, Joan Cole, Renée Flawn, H.W. (Joe) Hill, Andrew Lawrence, the late Herbert Males, Joan Oakesmonger, John Rivaz, David Robertson and Ruth Wainwright. I am also indebted to Ted Barker for permission to reproduce a number of his exquisite line drawings of local scenes. To all the others, too numerous to mention individually, who have contributed directly or (through their encouraging remarks) indirectly I am equally grateful.

Radlett in 1796 — from a water colour by an unknown artist, now in the
British Library.

The Lie of the Land

The civil parish of Aldenham — that is, in broad terms, the combined ecclesiastical parishes of Radlett and Aldenham — has a current population of around 10,000, of whom some four-fifths live in the principal settlement of Radlett (a mainly twentieth-century growth point); the remainder are scattered among the more ancient villages of Aldenham and Letchmore Heath and the smaller dispersed settlements of High Cross, Round Bush, Kemp Row, Boyden's Hill, Aldenham Wood, Medburn and Theobald Street — the last four having virtually disappeared from present-day maps as individual locations. Over the past hundred years, a series of boundary changes has resulted in the loss of areas in the south and west of the Parish to Bushey, Elstree and Boreham Wood, while territory from St Stephens and Watford parishes has been added in the north, including parts of the Munden estate on the far side of the River Colne. Delrow, Hilfield and the hamlet of Patchetts Green are still within the ecclesiastical parish of Aldenham, although excluded from the civil parish (and so from this history). In sum, therefore, Aldenham Parish over the years has comprised a more complex series of historic local settlements than might at first be imagined.

The whole of the present Aldenham Parish lies within the area of the London Green Belt: a providential creation which has prevented it from being swallowed up in the outward spread of the capital. That undoubtedly would have happened in the 1940s, had not the war intervened to stop further development and then the post-war Green Belt legislation effectively placed a *cordon sanitaire* around the perimeter of the metropolis.

The pre-war plans of London Transport provided for a further extension of the Northern Line northwards from Edgware to a new terminus at a station to be called Bushey Heath, which would have been located near Aldenham Reservoir on the southern limit of the parish boundary. Indeed, the 1940 edition of the Geographia Greater London road atlas showed this extension as a reality, with intermediate stations on the extension also marked in at Brockley Hill and Elstree. Some relics of the preliminary building works for this extension can still be seen near the site of the intended Brockley Hill station at the foot of the hill.

Having escaped by a whisker the threat of wholesale urbanisation, such as had happened to the former villages of Stanmore, Edgware and Boreham Wood a generation previously, Radlett now happily enjoys the position of a 'specified settlement' within the Green Belt, with tightly-drawn boundaries all around it; these are secure so long as present policies towards the preservation of the countryside last. The rest of the Parish of Aldenham, being wholly within the Green Belt, is similarly protected from further development other than for those uses compatible with this status. Further protection has been given by the designation of conservation areas covering the central area of Radlett and the whole of the villages of Aldenham and Letchmore Heath, the hamlet of Round Bush, and the area around the old Delrow School and almshouses. It is, indeed, quite remarkable that such an unspoiled English parish should be found a bare 20 kilometres from Charing Cross: a fact appreciated by Radlett inhabitants, who insist that they are still living in a 'village', albeit a rather overgrown one. The generally verdant countryside and conservation areas are jealously guarded by the parishioners through their local Parish Council and amenity societies.

The separation from Greater London now delineated by the Green Belt is further emphasised by the structure of the landscape. Gentle hills to the south of the Parish, forming the rim of the South Hertfordshire Plateau, create a psychological rather than a physical barrier, an effect which is further enhanced by the changing nature of the geological formations beneath. The Eocene Clay of the north-west side of the London Basin gives way to the Cretaceous Chalk of the dip slope of the Chiltern Hills, almost bisecting the Parish on an east-west axis: although the fact that the clay overlaps the chalk, which lies about 30 metres from the surface at Aldenham, Letchmore Heath and Round Bush tends to conceal this change. The evidence is to be found more in the deep chalk pits that remain on the southern side of Radlett, and the earlier buildings of the village constructed with flints from these sources.

The terrain of the area is, however, largely determined by the superficial formations that lie on top of the base geology, especially the glacial deposits from the last Ice Age. Aldenham is near the southern extremity of the ice penetration, but there was still sufficient movement to carve out the defile in which Radlett lies, and to bring deposits of gravel and boulder clay to the locality, which has provided another source of local building materials. The local landscape was further shaped, after the ice retreated, by fast-running streams which cut deeply into the easily-eroded boulder clay, ultimately forming the course of the Tykeswater stream, which drains the higher ground to the south and runs northwards through the valley at Radlett before joining the River Colne near Colney Street.

A unique feature of the locality is the presence of Hertfordshire Puddingstone. This is a conglomerate rather than a pure stone, but unlike any other, with rounded flint pebbles in a matrix where no pebble even touches the next. This rare rock was formed about 80 million years ago, when an earlier ice age brought flints from the Chilterns, rounded them and dropped them over a beach when the sea came up to Elstree. This beach was then covered by the sea and a great depth of soil which contained a heavy deposit of silica. The period was wet and warm, which resulted in the silica forming a matrix into which the rounded flint pebbles were cemented together. These deposits form part of the narrow, but important, band of Reading Beds which lie along the junction of the Cretaceous Chalk and the Eocene Clay and which contain pebbles, sands and shales and hold water, resulting in extensive ponds at Letchmore Heath, Otterspool and Piggott's (now Bhaktivedanta) Manor. Subsequent erosion wore away the deposits over the puddingstone and finally revealed these geological rarities around Aldenham and Radlett. Puddingstone is an immensely hard rock, which has the misfortune to look rather like modern man-made concrete aggregate. Because of its rarity and the difficulty of working it, not much has been used for building purposes, but it was employed in the construction of Aldenham Church tower in the fifteenth century, some buildings around Batlers Green and the walls of gardens in Gills Hill Lane and Aldenham Avenue in Radlett.

Netherwylde Farm, Radlett, drawn by Ted Barker.

The London Transport 1920s map of the area.

ABOVE: Model of small updraught pottery kiln dating from the third century, the remains of which were discovered near Loom Lane, Radlett in 1898. Key to lettering on model: A Stokehole pit; B Flue passage; C Combustion chamber; D Clay buttress; E Vent-holed oven floor of baked clay and F Temporary oven roof of turf and branches. (VM) BELOW: Roman mortarium and bowl excavated in Radlett. (VM)

Genesis

Looking at the peaceful open fields which make up most of the Parish of Aldenham, it would be easy to assume that this microcosm of the English rural scene has existed since time immemorial. Yet the reality is rather different. Until the Middle Ages, and in common with much of the rest of south-east England, most of the land was densely forested; the heavy, sticky soil beneath the trees gave little incentive to whatever people roamed the forests to clear it, so as to create a settlement based on agriculture. Only gradually in later ages has the predominantly oak forest been cleared, until today there are only vestigial traces left, such as the band of oaks to the north of the Parish (recorded in the name of Oakridge Avenue).

It can be no more than speculation that there was any settlement within the area of today's parish before Anglo-Saxon times. Certainly the earliest identifiable inhabitants of the areas north of the Thames, a Belgic tribe known as the Catuvellauni, who settled in parts of what is now Hertfordshire in about 80 BC, made attempts to clear parts of the primeval forest. Various settlements have been identified in places not many miles away. Since they had invaded the country from Roman-occupied Gaul by way of the Thames Valley, and had penetrated northwards as far as St Albans and Wheathampstead, where their leader, Cassivellaunus, built his capital, it is fair to assume that some roamed the local scene in search of subsistence. It also seems probable that they used the valley formed by the Tykeswater stream as a line of communication on their northwards advance: the precursor of the Roman route. But no archaeological traces have been found to indicate anything more than a transitory camp was created.

The Romans, too, throughout their period of occupation seemed to have hurried through the Aldenham area as quickly as they could, *en route* for the important city of Verulamium and staging posts further north. When Julius Caesar landed in 54 BC he probably forded the Thames at Brentford and then made tracks northwards to subdue the Britons at Wheathampstead and another fortified camp in Prae Wood, then known as Verlamion, just north of present St Albans. It would be natural to use any pre-existing tracks and, with a process of continuing use over the following centuries, the course of what later became known as Watling Street was formed, running as it still does today in a virtually straight line between the bottom of Elstree Hill and the outskirts of St Albans (where it originally carried straight on towards one of the gates of Verulamium).

Although the line of Watling Street is undoubtedly Roman, this name was not given to it until well after the Roman period. Some considerable time after the Romans had left Britain, old Verulamium became the headquarters of a Saxon tribe, the Waeclingas. Still using the ancient line of communication towards London, this became known first as Waeclingas-Streat and then, much later, as Watlynge Strata. By the thirteenth century, the modern form of Watling Street had been adopted.

One of the most important raw materials in the Roman domestic economy was clay, used for the bricks with which most important buildings were constructed and for the pottery used extensively in Roman homes. Since clay, perforce, had to be worked near the extraction site, it is not surprising

15

that substantial evidence of individual pottery works, remote from major settlements but near lines of communication, has been unearthed. The value of the pockets of brick earth in the gravelly beds covering the chalk of south-west Hertfordshire was quickly recognised, and the Street from Brockley Hill to Verulamium became flanked by numerous pottery kilns. Two such kilns were set up about 300 metres west of the Street near the present-day Loom Lane in Radlett, probably in the third century. Associated relics were discovered in 1898 during gravel extraction, but unfortunately workmen severely damaged the remains of the kilns (having mistaken them for land drains) before the importance of their find was realised. A number of domestic pots, jug-shaped amphorae and various forms of paterae were, however, preserved, most of them in the Verulamium Museum. Several of the artefacts were stamped with the name of the maker: CASTUS, or CASTUS FECIT ('Castus made it'). The evidence indicates that the kilns had been abandoned hurriedly, since the fires had been damped down and pots left in the kiln.

It has been suggested that another Roman road crossed the Aldenham area. A group of researchers calling themselves The Viatores, in their book *Roman Roads in the South-East Midlands*, listed 'Road 169' as running from Elstree to Eaton Bray in Bedfordshire. This would have left Watling Street a little to the south of the crossroads in Elstree village, heading northwards towards Letchmore Heath and Aldenham and passing through the grounds of Aldenham House and Aldenham School *en route*. It was hypothesised that the long, narrow bank running south of Aldenham Home Farm formed part of this road, the evidence for which was strengthened by the discovery in 1878 of a large quantity of broken Roman pottery a few feet below the surface, when a swimming pool was being excavated at Aldenham School. However, the bank is more likely of medieval origins, and no evidence of a road was found during excavations across its presumed line.

More recently, evidence of a substantial Roman dwelling has been discovered in excavations near the northern boundary of the Parish, in the Colne Valley at Netherwylde Farm. Structures so far identified include a bath-building, corridors and other parts of a dwelling house, a barn and a tile kiln. Roman tiles have also been unearthed in other scattered parts of the Parish, including Hill Farm, Little Munden Farm, Blackbirds Lane, Kemprow Farm, High Cross, Round Bush and near Aldenham Grange. There is also evidence that a Roman villa existed near Munden.

The first indications of settlement in the Aldenham area come from the sixth century, by which time Hertfordshire was included in the Kingdom of the East Saxons. It is possible that a tribal leader called Aelde formed a community or 'ham' around ponds found near Edge Grove. What is more certain is that the lands around Aldenham had so increased in value by the eighth century to become the subject of a continuing and seemingly bitter dispute, between the two major landowners: the Abbots of the newly-founded monasteries of St Albans, and of St Peter on Thorney Island, later to become Westminster Abbey. Among the Saxon charters preserved at Westminster Abbey is one dated 785, which purports to say that King Offa of Mercia (who founded St Albans Abbey in 793) granted the lands of Aldenham to the Abbot and monks of St Peter's, in return for a gold amulet. There is, however, a growing belief among scholars that the charter could be a forgery, dating from much later, possibly the tenth century. The document defines the boundary of what is the first reference to 'Aeldenham' as marked by Watling Street to the east and the Colne to the north; the other boundaries are not so clearly identifiable, but they broadly coincide with the Parish boundaries as they were later recorded, until the adjustments of the nineteenth century. Thus the 'Offa' Charter, whether of the eighth or tenth century, is a key stage in the evolution of Aldenham. There have also been suggestions that a Saxon church was established on the site of the present Aldenham Church in King Offa's time — though any evidence must lie below the present foundations.

The land to the east of Watling Street was originally, and for much of recorded history, administered separately from that to the west. Its first name was Titeberst, apparently covering territory as far east as Shenley and parts of Ridge. The origins of the name are uncertain, but the first element may reflect the Saxon personal name *Tit(t)a* and the second comes from Old English *geberst*, meaning an earth crack: a possible reference to the character of the clay soil.

The first documentation of the area comes from the Domesday record of 1086, which confirms that most land was then in the possession of the Abbot of Westminster, though parts of Titeberst were claimed by St Albans. The two major tenants of the Abbots were listed as Geoffrey de Mandeville and Geoffrey of Bec, who in turn leased parts of their holdings to villagers.

The several references in the Domesday entries to woodland, and to the large number of pigs associated with this woodland, indicate that the rural economy was still dominated by the forested nature of the local terrain; the relatively small amount of ploughed land was mainly on higher ground in the south-west, where the soil was more easily drained and the trees cleared.

The conflicting claims and feuding between the Abbots of Westminster and St Albans over the title of lands in Aldenham persisted well into the thirteenth century, probably only finally settled when the monasteries were dissolved by Henry VIII. According to the records of St Albans Abbey it was Abbot Leofstan in the eleventh century who cleared the thick woodlands between the Chilterns and London in the vicinity of Watling Street, making bridges, smoothing down the rough places and making safe the roads. Subsequent entries in the court books make it clear, however, that this process was not completed until much later. It is significant that the name 'Newland' or one of similar meaning appears frequently in the records, at least twice as the name of a manor and many times among field names.

Cussans in his *History of Hertfordshire* of 1879 says that 'the Abbot of Westminster brought a suit against his brother of St Albans for that the latter had on Tuesday after Pentecost in the year 1249 taken 15 beasts from Westminster Manor of Aldenham and driven them to the Manor of Parkbury in St Albans, and again on St John's Day in the same year had in like manner taken three other beasts. At the trial, St Albans asserted that the then King had confirmed to their abbey a proportion of the fines coming to the Crown on the circuits of the King's Judges within the Liberty of St Albans, a privilege they had held from time immemorial. This matter appears to have been settled out of court'.

Further disputes between the two abbots led to an elaborate final concord in the year 1256. Among various detailed statements on the distribution between them of the perquisites of justice in Aldenham it was laid down that the township of Aldenham should do suit to the hundred of Cashio, wherever it should be held, every three weeks, with a penalty of four shillings for every default in attendance. The tenants of the Abbot of Westminster were to be kept in his prison if arrested for crime, and tried at Aldenham before the bailiff of St Albans by other free men of the hundred and manor, and thieves condemned at Aldenham were to be hanged on a gallows common to both abbots. The township of Aldenham was to come with the three neighbouring vills, if necessary, to serve on coroners' inquests. Once a year the bailiff of the hundred was to hold the view of frankpledge at Aldenham. The procedure in serving and returning Royal courts was also laid down.

The gallows were erected 'in a certain spot called Keneprowe': an early version of Kemp Row, and almost certainly derived from the name of Richard Canap who, in the thirteenth century, held ten acres of land from the Abbot of Westminster at a rent of 4d. Kemp Row is on high ground next to ancient routeways linking Aldenham with St Albans. It would have offered a suitable vantage point for the public to observe and heed the results of the due process of law, including the penalty for such a heinous crime as unlawfully taking a fish from abbatial waters.

In about 1250, the Church of Aldenham was built (or perhaps rebuilt on the site of an earlier Saxon church). Only fragments of the original building remain, the present nave dating from the fourteenth century. The tower was probably begun in the thirteenth century, but not completed until the fifteenth. The first incumbent, Roger, was installed in 1267.

Throughout the medieval period, the principal landowners and lords of the Manor of Aldenham remained the Abbots of Westminster. They did not run the farms directly, but let out the lands to freemen and customary tenants (villeins). In an Extent of Aldenham Manor dating from around 1260, which has survived (and is now in the County Records Office), there is a list of tenants showing the amount of land held and the value of the rents paid. This is by far the most comprehensive listing of Aldenham inhabitants prior to the introduction of parish registers in the sixteenth century. 21 free tenants and about 60 customary tenants are detailed. Most of the holdings were of 10 acres or less. The list includes a number of tenants who gave their personal names to local place-names, mostly still in use today: Robert Boyden (Boyden's Hill); Richard Canap (Kemprow); Robert atte Delle (Delrow); John Page (Page's Farm); William Pachet (Patchett's Green); Reynold de la Penne (Penne's Place); Geof. Picot (Piggott's Manor); Ralph le Porter (Porter's Park); Gaburd de Walehale (Wall Hall).

To look after monastic interests, and to ensure the villeins carried out services laid down by the court, a local steward (known as a reeve) was appointed: he also collected the fines prescribed for non-compliance with manorial duties. Some of the minister's accounts maintained by Westminster Abbey during the thirteenth and fourteenth centuries have been preserved among the Abbey records: these include details of rents collected by the reeve and payments made to him for various maintenance services.

In the first preserved account, dated 1278, payments for repairs to the gate of the 'grange' are listed. Further references to the grange and a hall appear in later accounts, but these do not signify a manor house. The grange was a manorial building near the Church probably maintained for the abbot's steward or other official on his periodic inspections; the hall would have been used for moots and manorial courts. There were laid down the services which land-owners owed their lord; complaints were heard and fines imposed. Under the manorial system it was the local freemen themselves who dealt with these matters, usually with the reeve presiding.

The ministers' accounts also record repair and renewals of the 'mill', first recorded in the Domesday survey. This water mill was on the River Colne, probably at Otterspool, provided by the manorial authorities for the tenants to grind corn (for which a due was extracted). The first reference to a 'shop' — presumably a craftsman's workshop — comes more than a century later in 1398, with the receipt of rent from Thos. Neal 'for a certain parcel of the site of the manor next the church of Aldenham lying in length between the gate of the aforesaid manor and a certain shop by the same'.

The tenant farmers did not live in nucleated village communities, as was becoming increasingly the case in lowland England during the Middle Ages, but in the more ancient tradition (inherited from the Saxons) of dispersed farmstead settlements, adjacent to some of their field strips, and scattered around the periphery of the great area of common land which made up a substantial part of the southern and western area of the Parish. Originally completely forested, Aldenham Common would have formed a valuable addition to the tenants' land rights by providing a host of small necessities, ranging from summer grazing and faggots for fuel to hazel sways for thatching and bracken for pig litter. The use of the common land was strictly regulated and commoners' rights jealously guarded. In Aldenham Manorial Rolls of the early sixteenth century, for example, it is recorded that William Warner was fined 26s 8d for feeding too many beasts on the common and John Beaston fined 6s 8d 'for making a pit in the common and not filling it up as he was commanded'.

Scarcely any other records exist of buildings or the population in Aldenham Parish in the Middle Ages. One partially documented exception is the medieval moated homestead of Edmonds, on land now belonging to Batlers Green Farm. The earliest mention of this was in 1328, when it was probably in the possession of a John Edmond (who, in 1362, is recorded as having granted a messuage and garden to Hugh, son of Richard le Whighte of Ridge). In 1480, the will of John

Werall, Coroner and Attorney to Henry VII, bequeathed all his land in Aldenham including 'the manor called Edmondes' to his son, Ralph, with some income from this manor to be disbursed in other ways. In the 1960s, the site of Edmonds was excavated by members of the Watford & South West Hertfordshire Archaeological Society, uncovering the remains of the thirteenth century dwelling and farm buildings. These indicated a substantial main building with flint walls 33in. thick (of reused Roman material) supporting a timber-framed structure with wattle panels and clay-daub walls, surrounded by a moat and ramparts typical of the fortified homesteads of the period, but the excavations failed to date the complex with any precision.

There are records of at least two other medieval moated homesteads within the Parish — Penne's Place and Kendals — and other manorial sites at Aldenham, Letchmore Heath (Piggott's Manor), Aldenham Wood (Wigbournes), Newberries, Wall Hall and Munden, but tantalisingly little physical evidence in most cases as to the type of building associated with them.

Towards the end of the pre-Reformation period and arising from a legacy from Ralph Penne of Penne's Place, who died in 1485, his successor Sir Humphrey Coningsby built in 1510 a chapel on Coppidthorne (Cobden) Hill 'for the consolation of Christ's faithful and especially for the infirm, and for men and women broken with age, and women who have infants, who dwell far from the parish church'. In 1513, Coningsby was granted a licence to found a perpetual chantry for one chaplain in his chapel, for celebration of holy Eucharist, with the right to acquire lands to the annual value of £8 for its upkeep. This outpost of worship was justified by the many robberies on the journey to Aldenham, and break-ins while the faithful were away at worship. The robbers allegedly came from 'a suspect place called Busshey Heth'. Although the chantry survived the religious reforms of Henry VIII, it was dissolved in 1552, along with all other such relics of catholicism, on the orders of Edward VI, the endowments converted to 'good and godly use in the creating of Grammar Schools'. Buildings have existed on the site of the chapel ever since, the present Chantry Cottage, with its chapel-like appearance, dating from the beginning of the nineteenth century.

The Oak Ridge, Radlett, drawn by Ted Barker.

Manuscript purporting to be a charter of King Offa of Mercia from AD 785, granting land in Aldenham to Westminster Abbey; now believed to be a forgery dating from 10th or 11th century. (WA)

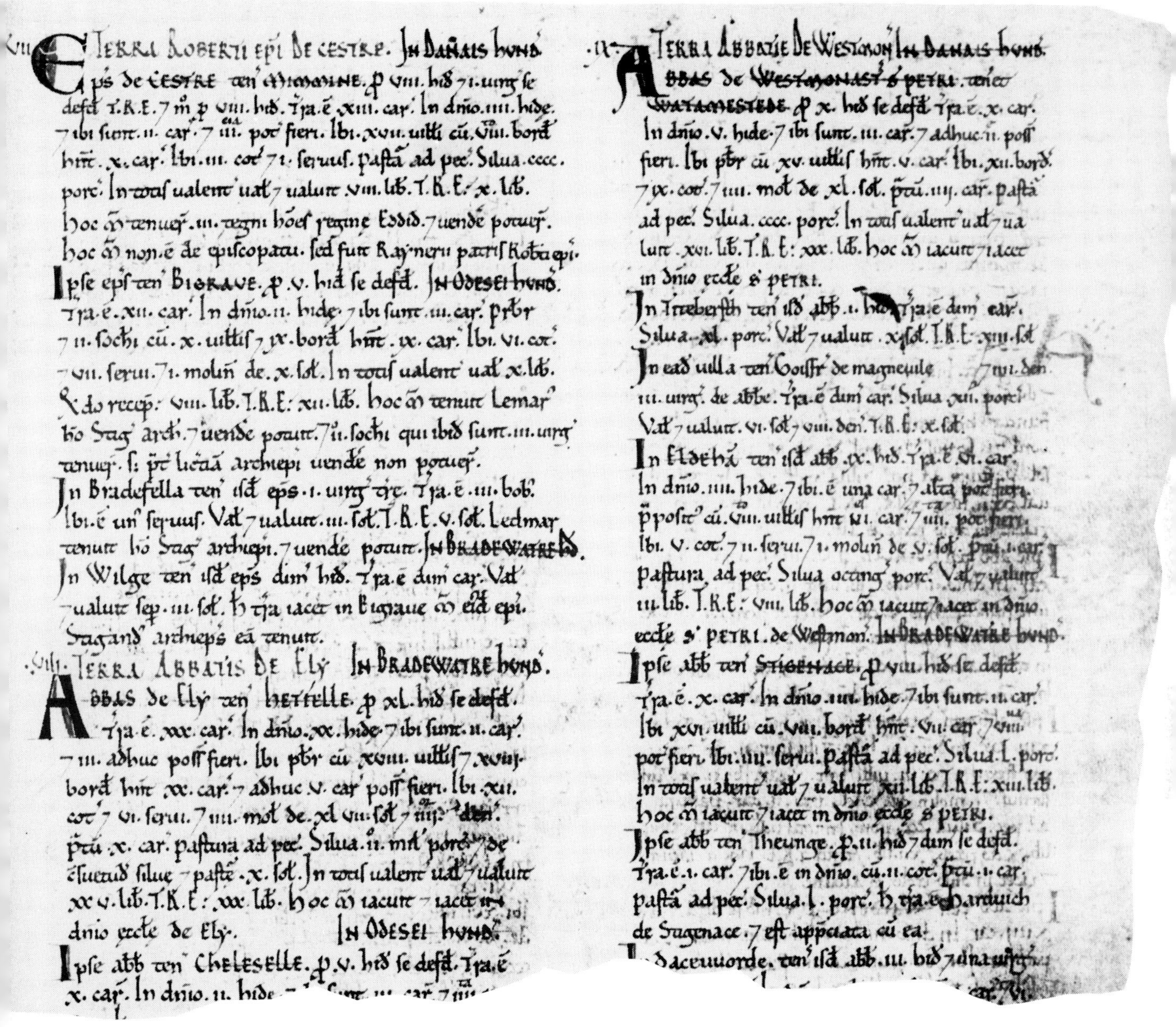

Extract from *Domesday Book*, 1086, recording (in the right-hand column) details of land in Hertfordshire held by the Abbey of Westminster. The second and third entries relate to land now in the Parish of Aldenham and in translation from the Latin shorthand read as follows:

'In Titberst (Theobald Street) the Abbot holds 1 hide. Land for ½ plough. Woodland, 40 pigs. The value is and was 10s; before 1066, 13s 4d.

'In the same village, Geoffrey de Mandeville holds 3 virgates from the Abbot. Land for ½ plough. Woodland, 12 pigs. The value is and was 6s 8d; before 1066, 10s'

'In Aldenham the Abbot holds 9 hides. Land for 6 ploughs. In lordship 4 hides; 1 plough there; a second possible. A reeve with 8 villagers have 3 ploughs; a fourth possible. 5 cottagers; 2 slaves. 1 mill at 5s; meadow for 1 plough; pasture for the livestock; woodland, 800 pigs. The value is and was £3; before 1066, £8. This manor lay and lies in the lordship of St Peter's Church, Westminster.' (PRO)

(Note: a 'hide' was a Norman unit of land equivalent to about 120 acres; a 'virgate' was a quarter of a hide, or 30 acres. A 'plough' comprised both the implement and the oxen, usually eight in number, which pulled it.)

21

ABOVE: Kemp Row, near Aldenham c1910: the medieval gallows erected jointly by the Abbots of Westminster and St Albans stood hereabouts. Note the coal-duty marker post denoting the Parish boundary and the point at which duty on coal being brought into the London area became payable. BELOW: Chantry Cottage on Cobden Hill. The present building, dating from c1800, stands on or near the site of the chantry chapel erected by Sir Humphrey Coningsby in 1510 and dissolved in 1552.

Lords of the Manor

When Henry VIII dissolved the monasteries in 1539 to boost Royal income, their lands in Aldenham became available to the highest bidder. The lordship of the manor of Aldenham and the lands that went with it were sold in 1547 to Ralph Stepneth (or Stepney) for £980. In 1557, a letter was issued 'to all and sundry' that Ralph Stepneth, Joan his wife and the heirs of Ralph and their men and tenants of the Manor of Aldenham were to be quit of taxes due throughout the realm in accordance with a grant by charter of Edward the Confessor to Edward, Abbot of Westminster.

Ralph Stepneth died in 1558 and was buried in the chancel of Aldenham Church. He was succeeded by his son, John, who in 1568 alienated the manor to his brother Robert. He was succeeded in turn by his son, Paul, who in 1588 sold the manor, with the rectory and advowson of the vicarage, to Sir Edward Cary.

The Stepneths appear to have been as autocratic as any other Tudor lord, judging from a dispute which arose in 1576 over the extent of common ground. The lord maintained it amounted to only 1,000 acres, whereas the commoners who signed a Bill of Complaint held it was more like 2,000. The dispute was settled in favour of Stepneth, who celebrated by enclosing 50 acres for his personal use and building a manor house soon afterwards, on a site near Aldenham Church, marked today by some mounds at the east end of Bowling Green Field. (The name perhaps identifies a previous pastime of the lords of the manor.) A farm near the site was called the Place Farm (now Church Farm), so the manor house was probably called Aldenham Place.

The Stepneth's successor, Edward Cary, was a Groom of the Privy Chamber at the court of Elizabeth I, Keeper of Marylebone Park and Master of the Jewel-House. He was knighted in 1596. He also held the lease of Berkhampstead Castle and was later granted the Manor of Hunslet, near Leeds, though he lived at Aldenham. He married the Dowager Lady Paget, widow of the second Baron Paget, and produced several children who, on his death in 1618, succeeded to his various properties.

Cary's eldest son, Henry, who was born in Aldenham and inherited the manor, was a courtier as well as a Member of Parliament for Hertfordshire. He was created Viscount Falkland in 1620 prior to being appointed Lord Deputy of Ireland 1622–27. Despite his considerable fortune he was constantly short of money, and in 1618 sold his inherited office of Master of the Jewel-House as well as persuading his wife to mortgage her own property. His marriage was not, in fact, a happy one. He had married Elizabeth, the daughter and heiress of Sir Laurence Tanfield, Lord Chief Baron of the Exchequer, in 1600 when she was only 15. Four years later she secretly became a Roman Catholic, a fact which she did not confess to her husband until twenty years later in Dublin, when in 1625 they separated. Shortly before the separation Lady Falkland had petitioned King James I to help her husband: 'My reasons are 9 children not unhopeful all designed to His Majesty's Service either by serving him themselves or to bring forth servants for him; my Lord himself hath before his birth served the King's predecessors and in his own person been a follower to three princes'. After the separation she was sometimes in real want, receiving little from her husband and cut off by her father for her earlier improvidence.

Henry Cary died in 1633 after a fall out hunting on the Royal estate at Theobald's Park, and was buried with his father in Aldenham Church. He was succeeded by his son, Lucius, the second Lord Falkland, who by all accounts — and rather in contrast to his father — was a paragon of virtue, an ornament to the nation and the envy of the age, despite (or perhaps because of) his youth. Born in 1610, he had already at the age of 19 inherited estates at Great Tew and Burford from his grandfather, and was therefore a major landowner. Throwing himself into politics, he became Member of Parliament for Newport, Isle of Wight in 1640. According to Lord Clarendon, he was 'a man of prodigious parts both natural and acquired, of untouched reputation in point of integrity, of inimitable sweetness and delight in conversation, and of such goodness to mankind as could hardly be equalled'.

When the Civil War broke out in 1642, Lord Falkland at first supported the Parliamentary party, but soon transferred his allegiance to the King, becoming his Secretary of State. He fought with the King at Edgehill and at the seige of Gloucester, but was killed at the first battle of Newbury in 1643 at the age of 33.

Shortly before his death, Falkland sold the Manor of Aldenham to raise funds for the Royal cause. The buyer was Sir Job Harby, Commissioner of the Customs, who was later created a baronet by Charles II. During his time as lord of the manor, he became embroiled in a dispute over the Aldenham benefice, which had been sequestrated by Parliament. Harby set up his own nominee in Thomas Horwood who, however, was represented to Parliament as: 'malignant, scandalous and very unfitting for the place, the parish being very great and wide, and near a thousand [!] communicants very ignorant'. It was further alleged that 'he hath lived in the King's quarters during the difference between King and Parliament; that he had been very active to withdraw man's hats and affections from the Parliament to syde with the King's partye, and so went up and down to p'swade men; that he had carried himselfe verry superstitiously amongs us in kneeling down to his devotion upon the stairs leading up to the pulpit when he went up to preach in the time of publique dutye'.

It was held against Sir Job that he was a 'discourager of those Godly ministers which the honourable Parliament hath placed amongst us in not paying their dues, and will show them no countenance; that he had been very urgent to have the Common Prayer read; a great countenancer of malignant ministers which Parliament had cast out; and was the very cause of Mr Horwood, whose malignancy would appear being placed amonst them'. Despite the rumpus, Sir Job did not have to leave his Manor because of his Royal leanings and, when he died in about 1664, it passed to his son, Erasmus, who disposed of it to Denzil Holles, the second son of John Holles, first Earl of Clare.

Denzil Holles had entered Parliament in 1624 at the age of 25, and became a leading protagonist in the constitutional struggle with Charles I. He achieved lasting celebrity as one of the 'five members' accused by the King of high treason. When Charles, accompanied by swordsmen, entered the Commons to arrest them, he discovered 'all the birds are flown'. They had taken refuge in the City, and a week later returned triumphantly to the House. Like many others prominent in the Parliamentary cause, Holles refused to go along with the more extreme policies of Cromwell and fled to France. At the Restoration he returned to England, was created Lord Holles of Ifield in 1661 and then served as Ambassador in Paris from 1663 to 1667.

Lord Holles is best remembered in local affairs for his intervention in the proposal by the governors of Aldenham School to turn the small Elizabethan grammar school into a free school for the education of the poor boys of the parish and to establish a new grammar school in Watford. A bill to achieve this was drafted and read a first time in the House of Lords, but withdrawn owing to the 'obstruction' of Holles, who objected to having Aldenham money spent on Watford, thereby condemning Aldenham School to a further 200 years of hand-to-mouth existence before it blossomed, in Victorian times, into the prominent public school it is today. On his death in 1679, the manor of Aldenham was held briefly first by his son, Francis, and then his grandson, Denzil, who died young, the title expiring with him in 1693.

The manor then passed to a distant cousin, John, fourth Earl of Clare, who was created Duke of Newcastle in 1694. The Duke is reputed to have pulled down Aldenham Place without rebuilding it. It is unlikely that either he, or his successor Thomas, Lord Pelham (created Earl of Clare in 1714 and Duke of Newcastle in 1715) ever lived in Aldenham. Newcastle became actively involved in the affairs of Parliament, leading the 'broad-bottom administration' of 1744–54 jointly with his brother, Henry Pelham, and on his succession to the highest office of First Lord of the Treasury in 1754 he sold the manor to a merchant named Samuel Vandewall.

Where Samuel Vandewall lived is not clear. Wall Hall had not then been built and Piggotts Manor and Delrow were occupied by others. He died in 1772 and his wife, Martha, continued as the lord. Her stepson, Thomas Neate, who owned the manor for a few years only, sold it in 1799 to George Woodford Thellusson, second son of Peter Thellusson, a wealthy land-owner whose convoluted will led to a famous lawsuit which lasted over fifty years (and was probably an inspiration to Charles Dickens in describing the seemingly never-ending case of Jarndyce vs Jarndyce in *Bleak House*). This suit obviously compelled George Thellusson to make over the manor to the trustees of his father's will, excepting Wall Hall, which he had built around the nucleus of an old farmhouse, and where he lived until his death in 1811. It was then put up for sale by public auction, although the lordship of the manor remained with the family. In 1803 the last of the common lands of the Parish were enclosed and added to the holdings of local land-owners.

Peter-Isaac Thellusson, the eldest son of Peter Thellusson, had been made a peer in 1806 with the title of Baron Rendlesham (after the name of an estate he possessed in Essex). He died two years later and was succeeded in the barony by his eldest son, John, who inherited the right to the manor of Aldenham in 1812; his third son, William (who had been Vicar of Aldenham for seven years before his inheritance), in 1832; and his fourth son, Frederick, in 1839. Frederick managed to produce a son some years before he died in 1852, Frederick William Brook Thellusson, who thus became the fifth baron and lord of the manor that year.

In 1877, the fifth Baron Rendlesham sold the vicarage and advowson of Aldenham to Henry Hucks Gibbs, of Aldenham House, and thus started the break-up of the manor. The final disintegration came early this century, when the American financier, John Pierpont Morgan, bought the freehold of Wall Hall and later, other lands in Aldenham, including Church Farm and Batlers Green Farm. The Rendlesham connection with the manor then came to an end; by that time the significance of the title had finally disappeared with the passage of the Law of Property Acts of 1922 and 1925.

The other principal manors within the Parish were those of Titberst & Kendals, Piggotts, and Wall Hall, although it is doubtful that the last two ever possessed full manorial powers.

Some of the lords of the manor of Aldenham in the seventeenth and eighteenth century: LEFT: Henry Cary, first Viscount Falkland, 1618–1633, RIGHT: Denzil Holles, first Baron Holles of Ifield, 1664–1679, OPPOSITE: John, fourth Earl of Clare and first Duke of Newcastle, 1692–1711, and BELOW: Thomas Holles Pelham, second Duke of Newcastle, 1711–1754 (on left).

AN

A C T

FOR

Dividing, Allotting, and Incloſing the Open and Common Fields, Commons, and Waſte Lands in the Pariſh of *Aldenham*, in the County of *Hertford*.

WHEREAS there are within the Pariſh of *Alden-* ham, in the County of *Hertford*, and Dioceſe of *Lincoln*, certain Open and Common Fields, and a certain Open Common, called *Aldenham Common*, and other Commonable Lands and Waſte Grounds, containing in the Whole, by Eſtimation, Five Hundred Acres or thereabouts :

Preamble.

And whereas *George Woodford Thelluſſon*, Eſquire, is Lord of the Manor of *Aldenham* aforeſaid, and as ſuch is ſeiſed of the Soil of the Commons and Waſte Lands within the ſaid Manor, except ſuch Part or Parts thereof as is or are now veſted in the Company of Proprietors of the Grand Junction Canal, by virtue of an Act paſſed in the Thirty-ſixth Year of His preſent Majeſty's Reign :

And whereas *William Phillimore*, Eſquire, is Lord of the Manor of *Tibhurſt* and *Kendalls* (Part of which lies in the ſaid Pariſh of

A   *Aldenham*)

Preamble to the Aldenham Enclosure Act of 1803, which authorised the transfer of the remaining common land of the Parish to the ownership of the local lords of the manor, and the rationalisation of the land holdings.

ABOVE: Rear view of Aldenham House c1910, dating from the later 17th century but remodelled and extended in the 18th and much enlarged after 1868 by Henry Hucks Gibbs, later the first Lord Aldenham, who also added the 'incongruous' (according to Pevsner) tower on the left of the entrance front. The steps, flanked by statues, lead from the terrace to the south garden. LEFT: Henry Hucks Gibbs, first Lord Aldenham (seated) and his third son Kenneth Gibbs, the Vicar of Aldenham, in 1905. (HCRO) RIGHT: Statues of a fiddler and a female singer which flanked the terrace steps at Aldenham House. (LA)

In Great Estate

Following the break-up of monasterial holdings, Aldenham Parish became a mixture of traditional common land and enclosed estates. Originally the vast Aldenham Common occupied a large part of the southern area, but successive enclosures by land-owners reduced its scale until, by the end of the eighteenth century, only the Great Common Field adjoining Common Lane, and scattered areas of mainly grazing fields, woodland and wasteland remained.

In 1795, some 70 acres of the Common were acquired by the Grand Junction Canal company, to form the Aldenham Reservoir which, with an outlet *via* the Tykeswater stream flowing through Radlett, fed water into the River Colne to make good supplies depleted by the canal's locking system. This was a statutory requirement upon the company, to protect the long-established interests of millers along the banks. They were empowered to appoint a superintendent at Aldenham whose salary would be paid by the company. The reservoir was extended in 1801, but the need to keep the Colne abundantly fed has long since disappeared and today the reservoir performs a purely amenity function as part of the Aldenham Country Park.

The common land virtually disappeared at the beginning of the nineteenth century, when the lords of the manors of Aldenham, Titberst & Kendals and Piggotts got together to promote a bill authorising them to enclose all the 'Open and Common Fields, Commons, and Waste Lands' of the Parish. In 1803, Parliamentary Commissioners were appointed to survey the Parish and make recommendations. This led to a rationalisation of local land structure and ownership, including the stopping-up of many long-established roads and the creation of a number of new ones, and resulted in a pattern of land ownership which held good through the whole of the nineteenth century and which saw the heyday of the great estates.

The Aldenham House Estate
The history of this estate starts with the Penne family. In an Extent of the lands belonging to Westminster Abbey taken in 1272, Reginald de la Penne is recorded as a free tenant holding two acres. Much later, a John Penne is mentioned in a 'List taken in the reign of Henry VI of those who would dispend Ten Pounds per annum, and resident in the County'.

The last of the Penne line died in 1485, at which time Penne's Place comprised a building and 70 acres of land in Aldenham: the site of this building can still be traced in the grounds of Aldenham House. The estate passed to the Coningsby family, and some of its funds were used by Sir Humphrey Coningsby to fulfil a bequest in Ralph Penne's will that a chapel be founded on Coppidthorne (Cobden) Hill.

In 1640 the freehold was sold to Henry Coghill, a prosperous London merchant, once a tenant of Penne's Place and who had married Faith Sutton, the then owner of the neighbouring Tudor mansion of Wigbournes. Chauncy in 1700 referred to the estate as 'a small mannor situated upon the Common where Henry Coghill Esq. built a fair house of brick: he was constituted Sheriff for this county, 1632. Upon his decease it descended to Henry, his son and heir, sheriff 1673 and the present possessor'.

Coghill's 'fair house of brick', built about 1640 as a replacement for the old Wigbournes, formed the nucleus of the present mansion. It was generally occupied by younger members of the family, while Penne's Place remained the family seat for four generations of Henry Coghills. In 1735 the estate was inherited by the last Henry's daughter, Sarah, who five years previously had married Robert Hucks, a brewer who owned extensive property at Clifton Hampden in Oxfordshire. It was Sarah who changed the name to Aldenham House; she also installed the Venetian window to the left of the west front. Later, her son, Robert Hucks, made many additions, including the library; his work is commemorated on a stone tablet in the courtyard reading: 'These stables and improvements were begon and finish'd by Robert Hucks in the year 1785'.

Since the sixteenth century the estate had grown by the progressive enclosure of common lands, culminating in the Parliamentary enclosures of 1803. Meantime the old Penne's Place had degenerated into no more than a farmhouse, and latterly a ruin, whose remains were almost completely removed in time. After the death of Robert Hucks (unmarried) in 1814, the estate stagnated while it was owned by loosely connected members of the Hucks family. A number of early deaths thwarted intentions that it remain with those of Hucks-Coghill stock, and it was finally inherited in 1843 (together with the Clifton Hampden estate) by Henry Hucks Gibbs, the grandson of Antony Gibbs, who had founded the large banking firm that bears his name, and of which he himself was senior partner.

For the first twenty-five years of his inheritance, Henry Hucks Gibbs lived at the family home of Clifton Hampden but, with the coming of the local railway line in 1868, he decided to transfer to Aldenham. By now one of the wealthiest men in the country, Alderman and Member of Parliament for the City of London, and a future Governor of the Bank of England, Gibbs rapidly set about creating a country residence fitting for a man of his position. Having found the house in a 'neglected and somewhat dilapidated state' he employed various notable architects, including Sir Arthur Blomfield, to make large additions of which *Country Life* wrote in 1924 'may [they] one day be appreciated as they were at the time of their erection'. These included a vast new library to house his collection of more than 10,000 books.

During the next 60 years, Henry Hucks Gibbs, in 1896 created first Lord Aldenham, and his second son, the Hon Vicary Gibbs, between them turned Aldenham House into an opulent gentleman's country retreat and even more impressively the gardens into some of the finest in England. The hero of this latter enterprise was Edwin Beckett, head gardener to both generations and a man of distinctive achievement in horticulture. With more than 50 under-gardeners and apprentices, and unlimited funds, he set about this project in the 1880s and it was to occupy him for virtually all his long working life.

Beckett's ambition, fully realised during his tenure, was to create a show estate reputedly (and with probably only a little exaggeration) containing a specimen of every tree growing in the western hemisphere, including 150 different oaks, 300 berberis and an unbelievable 700 varieties of thorn. A border of Michaelmas daisies 'some 150 yards long and in places 15 yards wide' comprised 300 plants of 70 varieties, many over five feet tall.

In 1907, Aldenham was chosen from gardens throughout Europe to raise the seeds sent back from China by the horticulturist Ernest Wilson, and within two years, well-grown specimens of over 600 species and varieties were being sent to botanic gardens all over the world.

Apart from the many ornamental gardens and the huge walled kitchen garden, a series of water gardens were created, with 'rocks' and 'stone' bridges made out of a reconstituted stone known as Pulhamite. These were supplied with six million gallons of water a year piped from Aldenham Reservoir (intermittently interrupted when required for its original purpose of replenishing water taken by the Canal). A stretch of the Tykeswater stream which runs through the estate was widened into an ornamental lake.

This tremendous achievement came to an abrupt end in 1932 when Vicary Gibbs died, leaving behind a unique collection of trees and shrubs which compared favourably with the older collection at Kew. The Gibbs family, rather dismissive of 'Vicary's silly bushes', were disinclined to take on the huge financial responsibility involved in their upkeep and, although it was suggested that the gardens should be acquired for the nation, within six months of his death it was decided to sell off and disperse the entire collection. Eminent horticulturists travelled from throughout Europe to attend what has been described as 'the greatest garden sale in the world' comprising some 2,000 lots and which lasted a full seven days. At the end, only the more established trees too large to move remained, and a saddened Edwin Beckett retired to live out the few remaining years of his life in Radlett.

Aldenham House remained empty until 1934, when it was rented to a Brigadier Watkins, who turned it into a country club and 'Residential Health Resort' with a 52-acre nine-hole golf course laid out on the site of the girls' school. This was not a success and the estate languished until it was taken over by the BBC during the Second World War, as the headquarters of Latin-American and Near East radio services. Wartime stringency prevented the upkeep of the gardens and, by the end of the war, they suffered such total neglect that the Aldenham House Club brought an action against the BBC for gross negligence. Although substantial damages were paid, it was obviously impossible to restore the gardens. In 1951 the BBC bought the estate with a view to making it a permanent headquarters of the Overseas Service, but ideas soon changed when Caversham Park, Reading was chosen instead. Further plans to install television studios came to nothing, and in 1959 the BBC sold the estate, the grounds of which were by then much overgrown, to the Haberdashers' Company for the establishment of the present school, which had outgrown its previous cramped premises in north London. Today little remains of the past spectacular layout of the gardens, though much of the ground plan is readily traceable in the school grounds.

Kendals

Parish land to the east of Watling Street did not belong to the manor of Aldenham, but to an equally ancient manor known as Titberst & Kendals. Its origins and its boundaries have not been clearly established, but it is thought to have extended eastwards towards Shenley or even as far as Ridge at one time, and south from Harper Lane as far as Medburn. Titberst is mentioned six times in the great survey of 1086 and it is likely that there were two manors, each called Titeberst, belonging to the Abbots of St Albans and Westminster respectively, and that the land belonging to the former acquired the name of Kendals, after a thirteenth century land-owner called Jordan de Kendale. Following the seizure of the monasteries, the manor was annexed to the Duchy of Lancaster and remained part of the Crown lands until 1607, when James I granted 'the manor of Tidburst, in the County of Middlesex, and Kendall, in the County of Hertford', to Robert Cecil, first Earl of Salisbury, of Hatfield House; in whose family it remained until 1739, when it was sold by James, the sixth Earl, to William Jephson, a wine importer with offices in the City of London.

Jephson died childless in 1766; he and his wife are both buried in Aldenham churchyard. His estate, and the lordship of the manor, passed to Robert Phillimore, who had married his niece in 1743. Thus began the long association of the Phillimore family with the Parish of Aldenham, during which the family acquired further land to the west of Watling Street. By the middle of the nineteenth century, the Phillimore estate amounted to some 1,750 acres, including lands outside Aldenham Parish such as Salisbury Hall, Pinks Farm and Shenley Lodge. These, and the Newberries estate, were sold off during the second half of the century.

Robert Phillimore built the present Kendals Hall some time before the end of the eighteenth century, and died there in 1818. The manor passed through four more generations of Phillimores, each with the first name, William, by direct descent until William Brough Phillimore died childless in 1887. The estate then went to a third cousin, Sir Walter, later Lord Phillimore. Sir Walter, a lawyer and subsequently a Lord of Appeal, remained in his family seat at Henley-on-Thames and gave the manor of Titberst & Kendals to his eldest son, Robert Charles Phillimore, generally known as Bobby.

Bobby Phillimore was born in 1871; a serious illness in childhood denied him proper schooling, and left him with a weakness of the heart from which he never fully recovered. Nevertheless he became a social reformer, a Socialist and an active member of the Fabian Society. Along with Sidney Webb he represented Deptford on the London County Council for a number of years, and later stood (unsuccessfully) as a Liberal candidate for the Ripon division of Yorkshire in 1907 and for St Albans at the general election of 1910. J.E. Saul, in *Radlett Past and Present* wrote 'The welfare of the denizens of the teeming slums of the metropolis appealed strongly to his sensitive heart', and in 1898 he chaired the first meeting of the Workmen's National Housing Council formed by Fred Knee, another Radlett resident. Locally, Bobby Phillimore was responsible for the erection of several blocks of flats in Scrubbitts Square, which were let at low rents to the poorly paid manual workers of Radlett: an early example of philanthropic housing inspired by the work of the Peabody Trust in London. He also established a dairy there and later, while living in Batlers Green House during the First World War, he laid out orchards at The Fruit Farm off Common Lane, where some unemployed Bermondsey girls were trained in horticulture.

The Kendals estate started to be broken up from 1898, when parcels of land to the west of Watling Street were sold for housing development. Bobby Phillimore gave Scrubbitts Wood to the village and, after his premature death (before his father's), at Kendals Hall in 1919, his widow Lucy also gave it the Phillimore Recreation Ground.

In 1926 Lucy Phillimore ceased to live at Kendals Hall and the mansion and grounds were leased off over the years to various gentlemen of means, a Jewish country club and, finally in 1980, it was acquired by the Radlett Preparatory School. As with the manor of Aldenham, the lordship of the manor of Titberst & Kendals had long since ceased to have any significance.

Newberries

The origins of the Newberries estate are lost in antiquity, but it certainly existed in one form or another for at least 700 years. Its early history is obscured because the records are so mixed up with those of 'New' Organ Hall, but it is thought that the earlier buildings stood on the west side of Shenley Road, where the Home Farm buildings were later constructed, between the present Williams Way and Faggotts Close. Old Organ Hall lay to the south-west a few hundred yards away. About the beginning of the nineteenth century a Mr Towgood laid out grounds from 'Newberries' to 'New Organ Hall', but it was not until William Robert Phillimore, lord of the manor of Titberst & Kendals, purchased the estate in the 1830s, that the Hall was called Newberries.

The first established reference to the estate, then called 'Newbury', appears in the records of the St Albans Abbey for 1235 (*Gesta Abbatum Monasterii Sancti Albani*). In 1281 Richard Forester, the reeve appointed to oversee various services carried out by the customary tenants, received 9d for three quarters of faggots sold at 'Neuburi', and in 1287 he paid 5s 6d for the cutting of corn at the same place.

It is not until the start of the sixteenth century, by which time the St Albans Abbey interests appear to have been disposed of (in advance of the dissolution of the monasteries), that land-holders can be identified at all clearly. A Robert Louthe bequeathed the lands to his three sisters, who each conveyed her share in 1514 to Sir Humphrey Coningsby, who in 1548 conveyed the estate to Richard Howes. Later owners were Thomas Harmer and Sir Thomas Pickering, who sold it in the 1620s to Richard Brisco(e), a former Sherriff of Hertfordshire.

The Briscoes, who became linked by marriage to the Coningsbys, were prominent local land-owners for well over two hundred years. In 1629, Edward Briscoe organised a scheme for setting the poor to work at the spinning of linen and cloth, and continued an early allowance for this purpose which had been made by his father. He was described as 'of Titburst Street and

Newberries' when, six years later, he gave 6s 6d towards the relief of the poor, in return for which he obtained a licence from the Archbishop of Canterbury to eat flesh in Lent. Edward Briscoe died in 1636, and in a schedule the following year which listed his holdings this occurs:

'The Manor NEWBERRIES als. BONESBUSHES with appurtenances and one messuage and with the appurtenances called ORGAN HALL als. ORGAR HALL and adjoining lands meadows feedings and pastures to the said messuage belonging, parcel of the manor of NEWBERRIES . . . lying in the parish of ALDENHAM . . . and heretofore parcel of the Manor of TITBERST in the said County is holder of His Majesty as of his late Monastery of St Albans by fealty only and worth by the year above reprises £6:13:4.'

The quaint alternative name of Bonesbushes appeared for the first time in the Parish Register in 1627 when William Whitehead was baptised on 1 November. It may have derived from the discovery of a cache of human bones in the bushes or scrub.

The manor remained in the hands of the Briscoe family until 1739 when it was conveyed to Jonathan Winder. John Paddey and Nathan Perkyns were later occupiers, and the 1766 map of Hertfordshire made by Dury and Andrews lists Captain Durell as living at Newberries and Mr Kitson at New Organ Hall.

In 1791, Mr Towgood acquired both Newberries and New Organ Hall, and built the last house on the estate. In a Register of Electors dated 1832 W.R.F. Eyre is shown as the owner. In 1833 it was bought by William Robert Phillimore, great-great-grandson of Robert Phillimore, whose father-in-law, William Jephson had devised the Kendals estate to him in 1766, thus enriching a family of outstanding ability.

William Robert, who was High Sherriff in 1834, died in 1846, leaving the estate to his son, William Brough Phillimore, to whom Radlett largely owes its Parish Church. He was a captain in the 6th Dragoon Guards and later in the Grenadiers; he fought in the Crimea. He died childless in 1887.

Thomas Bagnall (1799–1885), who for a few years had lived at Aldenham Lodge and also helped to endow Christ Church, bought Newberries in 1870 from W.B. Phillimore, when the estate consisted of 205 acres, the latter retaining the Home Farm and its lands. In the 1871 census, Bagnall, then aged 71, is described as a magistrate and land-owner. There were then 19 people in the mansion. Besides Mr and Mrs Bagnall and their two adult, unmarried daughters there were 15 living-in servants: a butler, housekeeper, cook, footman, ladies' maids (2), housemaids (2), laundry maids (2), dairy maid, kitchen maid, grooms (2) and a page.

The next owner was Sir Francis Head (1817–87), who acquired the estate some time after 1881. His father, the first baronet, was a tough extrovert who had served in the Royal Engineers, managed a mining company in South America and later became Lieutenant Governor of Upper Canada. Sir Francis was obviously a chip off the old block; a great horseman, he continued riding to hounds to the time of his death.

According to J.E. Saul, Sir Francis Head was a great upholder of the rights of property and objected strongly to villagers straying from the public footpath across his park. If cottages on his estate became untenanted he straightaway pulled them down, and Lambeth Cottages (a pair of old thatched cottages on Shenley Hill), those behind Brickfield in Theobald Street, and a cottage and the park lodge at the old entrance to the estate on Watling Street (which had had to be abandoned when the railway cut across the park in 1865), were all demolished.

Head had let it be known that he did not wish to be buried in consecrated ground, and so on his demise in August 1887 his body was buried among the bushes in the shrubbery of Newberries: thus reviving the prophetic ancient name of Bonesbushes. Before Lady Head died in November of the same year, however, she had directed that they should be buried together in the newly-built Radlett cemetery, and so the late Baronet's remains were exhumed and came to rest by her side in the sarcophagus which is still a prominent feature of the churchyard today. It was the first interment in the cemetery, which had been consecrated only the previous day. The interment was carried out after dark by the light of 'some lanterns dimly burning' according to the recollection of the late William Wing, who stopped with his brother to witness the scene while walking back from Medburn School. With filial affection and piety, the Heads' two sons later built the brick wall which surrounds the cemetery, in remembrance.

The estate then passed into the hands of H.J. Lubbock DL (1838–1910), whose brother, the first Lord Avebury, was responsible for the institution of Bank Holidays. It was sold again in about 1903 to Mr George Miller, a merchant with extensive interests in Africa. Harold Knee recalls:
'Mr Miller spent large sums in improving the house, although when a wing was added it rather detracted from its architectural proportions. It was not a very large mansion but it had a pleasing appearance — it was mid-Georgian with well-detailed Venetian Windows — and was situated in some lovely parkland. Although its gardens were not of the finest there were pleasant walks, a rosary, long herbaceous borders and some fine trees. There were two lodges — South Lodge, at the entrance to the present Craigweil Avenue, and North Lodge on the west side of Williams Way.

'On Saturday afternoons all the world and his wife would climb Shenley Hill to loll on the grass, or sit in deck chairs, and watch the 'flannelled fools' at play on a pitch just inside the park on the east side of the drive, now Williams Way; an attractive looking thatched pavilion was put up there for the use of the players and one could always get a cup of tea, or some ginger pop, and a slice of cake or a bun. It was an idyllic spot for a cricket match.'

Unlike his predecessor, Sir Francis Head, Mr Miller seems to have encouraged the use of his grounds by the local community, by whom the estate was known and colloquially referred to as 'Miller's Park'. As well as its use by the Radlett Cricket Club, many fairs and charitable events took place in the grounds during his tenure.

A down-turn in Mr Miller's business interests caused him to put the estate on the market in the mid-'30s and it was purchased by Sir Arthur du Cros of Bognor Regis — he who lent his Craigweil House to King George V for the monarch to convalesce after a serious illness — who proceeded immediately to develop the land for housing. In order to attract purchasers of his plots he laid out a golf course with the mansion as its club house; its dining room was magnificent and the locker rooms and toilets sumptuous. The course, however, was short and cramped for space — there were five short holes — and a part of it was clayey. It did not last for long for, with the outbreak of war in 1939, it folded up and the mansion was let to the United Kingdom and Provident Insurance Company, for use by staff evacuated from offices in central London; eventually it was divided into flats.

By that time, developers William Old & Co had acquired the property and, after the war, new building proceeded apace. Sadly, in 1957, the house was demolished and 'finis' was written for Newberries which, under various guises, had been in existence for more than seven centuries.

Piggotts
Thomas Picot, of Norman descent, held land in Aldenham granted by the Abbot of Westminster in the twelfth century, and a small homestead was no doubt built on or about the site of the present manor house around that time. The subsequent descent and the status of Picot's Manor is uncertain until the fifteenth century, when the land was held by John Hale, citizen of London, whose elder daughter had married John Penne of Penne's Place and who later settled it on his grandson, Ralph Penne. On the latter's death the manor passed with the other Penne property to Sir Humphrey Coningsby, who in time disposed of it to Richard Hewes. Later, in 1570, it was granted to the Briscoe family, who already owned the Newberries estate and other local land.

Piggotts Manor (as it was by then called) remained with the Briscoes until 1718. After two further owners it was sold in 1794 to the Hon George Villiers, who was busily acquiring an estate to surround his new mansion of Hilfield Castle. Following the financial scandal which ruined Villiers, the estate was put on the market around 1810, described in the following terms:

'An elegant and convenient Manor consisting of a drawing-room, a library, painted glass windows, an alcove dining-room, servants' hall, kitchen, and domestic offices, four principal bed-chambers, closets, small bedroom, 4 large attics, and store-room, with principal and back stairs, the whole elegantly fitted up and in complete order, ample stabling, with lofts, double coach-house, farm-yard and buildings; spacious enclosed garden, well stocked with choice fruits; and Gardener's cottage, pleasure ground, including a handsome piece of water and shrubbery, with ornamental plantations, and sundry parcels of land totalling in all 106 acres.'

It was bought by a Mr McIntosh, but resold in 1832 to the Thellusson family, who had acquired the manor of Aldenham, and was later leased out to tenants. In 1884 it was bought by Mr G.W. Williams, who pulled down most of the house and built the present, larger one in mock-Tudor style; he also did much to improve the appearance of Letchmore Heath, by landscaping the area around the village green which faces the gates to the estate.

The manor changed hands in 1912 and again in 1931, by which time the estate amounted to some 122 acres. For a while it was occupied by Claude Graham-White, the pioneer aviator. Later it came into the possession of St Bartholomew's Hospital Group, which used it as a training centre for student nurses, but in 1973 it was purchased by George Harrison of Beatles fame, who donated it to the International Society for Krishna Consciousness for use as a residential theological college. After 800 years, the old name has now been changed to that of Bhaktivedanta Manor.

Wall Hall

The first recorded reference to this estate is in 1250, when Guy de Walehale disposed of some land at the 'court of Walehale'. A family called Saer held part of the property during the thirteenth century, and it is recorded that John Saer was indicted for sheep stealing in 1287 and put in the Aldenham stocks. By the authority of Richard II, the manor of Wall Hall was given to the Prior and Convent of Saint Bartholomew in Smithfield in 1392, and it remained in their possession until the dissolution of the monasteries.

From 1619, when the estate was purchased by Sir Henry Cary, first Lord Falkland and lord of the manor of Aldenham, the manor of Wall Hall had little independent existence, and the lands were leased out to farmers. It was not until George Woodford Thellusson bought the manor of Aldenham in 1799, and three years later sold all of it except Wall Hall to the trustees of his father's will, that the estate resumed its position as a separate manor.

Then the manor house was no more than a modest farmstead. Thellusson greatly enlarged the building and gave it the present mock-castellated exterior. On his death in 1811, Wall Hall was sold to Admiral Sir Maurice Pole, who had served in the Navy but later entered politics. Pole changed the name of the house to Aldenham Abbey and, to lend an air of realism, built some sham 'ruins' with stones from Aldenham Church. He died in 1831 shortly after being created Master of the Robes and Admiral of the Fleet by William IV. His widow continued to live there until her own death in 1842, when the estate passed to her eldest daughter, Henrietta, who was married to William Stuart, a Watford magistrate.

The Stuarts lived at Wall Hall from 1842 to 1874 and it was during their period that the portico was added to the front of the house, as well as the library, with its plaster-beam roof, and the conservatory. After the death of William Stuart the estate remained in the family although both his son and his grandson chose to live on another estate in Bedfordshire. For some time the property was leased to Charles Van Raalte, a wealthy stockbroker, but finally in 1910 the Stuarts sold it to Mrs Jane Norton Morgan of New York, wife of the well-known American financier, John Pierpont Morgan junior. Morgan purchased the estate through his wife largely to indulge his recreation of game-shooting, for which purpose he occupied the mansion — which he renamed Wall Hall — for no more than seven or eight weeks each year.

Although mainly an absentee landlord, Pierpont Morgan retained a large staff to look after the house and run the estate. After his wife died in 1925 he succeeded to the property. Despite his infrequent visits he took a great, and on the whole benevolent, interest in the local environment, bought up additional land and developed the village of Aldenham as part of his estate. In 1921 he established a flock of Southdown sheep which became of national importance. Most of the villagers were in his employ and, to encourage sobriety, he bought up the old Chequers Inn opposite the Church and turned it into a social club. During his periods of residence large house and shooting parties were held, George VI among his guests.

With the outbreak of the war in 1939, Morgan returned to the United States and the Hall was loaned to the American ambassador, Joseph Kennedy, who stayed there at weekends with his family, including his son John, a future President. Shortly before the war, Hertfordshire County Council had taken an option on the estate so that an open space might be provided on the east side of Watford (before the days of Green Belt policy). On John Pierpont Morgan's death in 1942 the sale went through. At that time the estate extended to well over 1,000 acres and included, as well as the mansion and its immediate grounds, the Home Farm, Blackbirds Farm, Church Farm, Batlers Green Farm and extensive woods near the River Colne with pheasant hatcheries, as well as Edge Grove and much of Aldenham village.

After various wartime usages, including that of a clandestine training centre for work with European underground movements, and as a maternity hospital, the mansion and some 54 acres of grounds were opened in May 1945 by the then Minister of Education, R.A. Butler, as the first emergency training college for women teachers. Later it became a normal teachers' training college administered by the County Council; today it forms part of the Hatfield Polytechnic. The farmlands are leased to various tenant farmers.

Munden

The whole of the Munden area of the Colne Valley shows signs of considerable Romano-British settlement. On the eastern slopes of the valley, shards of Roman tile have been found in various places, while on the west bank of the river the remains of a Roman villa have been found under the lawn of the house. A well-known barrow with cremation burials was situated about five hundred metres to the south-west of the house.

The name itself comes from the Saxon *mund*, a safe place, and *dene*, a valley. In the twelfth century it was known as Meriden and formed part of the possessions of the Abbey of St Albans; it came to the Crown at the Dissolution. The Watford family of Ewers, ancestors of the Hibberts, held the estate in 1609, when the earliest part of the present house was built. It then passed to John Rogers, merchant, and through him to the Hibbert family. The male line of the Hibberts died out but, under the terms of his grandmother's will, Arthur Henry Holland became the owner, subject to his assuming the name and arms of the Hibberts in addition to his own, which he did when he came of age in 1876. The Hon Arthur Holland-Hibbert became the third Viscount Knutsford (of Cheshire) when his twin brother, older by half-an-hour, died. The title had been awarded to their father, Henry Thurstan Holland, in 1895. The fourth and fifth Lords Knutsford continued to live at Munden but, on the recent death of the latter, the title passed to a cousin, and the house is now occupied by the sister of the late Viscount, the Hon Diana Holland-Hibbert.

The Munden estate, though somewhat smaller than in earlier days, still amounts to some 800 acres, only part of which is in the Parish. The house was altered in 1720 and refurbished twice in the nineteenth century; viewed from the Colne footbridge across the rising meadow land, it now stands as a modestly handsome mansion (and a much-loved home) well tucked away in the heart of the Holland-Hibbert domain.

ABOVE: Part of the water gardens at Aldenham House, featuring the
Pulhamite bridge, and BELOW: with the rustic bridge. (LA)

ABOVE: Part of the flower garden at Aldenham House, with carpet bedding scheme commemorating the Diamond Jubilee of Queen Victoria in 1897. (LA) BELOW: Edwin Beckett, head gardener at Aldenham House from the 1880s until 1932, with his 58-strong team of gardeners (many of whom spent their entire working life on the estate). (LA)

LEFT: Poster for the 1886 garden show. ABOVE: Vicary Gibbs' bedroom at Aldenham House in the 1920s: a curiously modest room for such a major land-owner. (RCHM) BELOW: Part of the Great Library at Aldenham House, designed by Sir Arthur Blomfield in 1884. (RCHM)

ABOVE: Newberries Hall in the early 1900s: this 'fine Mid Georgian mansion, with well detailed trim, Venetian windows etc' (Pevsner) was demolished in 1957 prior to the final stages of the development of the Newberries housing estate. BELOW: The stable block at Newberries in the 1920s; (SM) OPPOSITE ABOVE: the Miller family there in the 1920s, (IS) and BELOW: Mr John Sutherland and Mrs Lily Sutherland, butler and nanny in the 1930s. (IS)

ABOVE: Newberries: the hall and gallery; (SM) OPPOSITE ABOVE: the
corner of drawing room, (SM) and BELOW: the first floor landing. (SM)

42

ABOVE: Newberries: the south gate and lodge from Theobald Street. The drive forms the line of the present Craigweil Avenue; BELOW: greenhouses and kitchen garden; (SM) OPPOSITE ABOVE: the approach drive to the Hall, (SM) and BELOW: an aerial view of the estate c1935.

The Particulars

OF THE VERY

ELIGIBLE FREEHOLD ESTA'

PRINCIPAL PART TITHE-FREE,

AND LAND-TAX REDEEMED,

COMPRISING THE

MANOR, or REPUTED MANOR of WALL H...

LATE THE PROPERTY AND RESIDENCE OF

George Woodford Thellusson, Esq. M.P. Deceased,

THE

ELEGANT FAMILY MANSIC

With Castellated Fronts,

WELL PLANNED OFFICES OF ALL DECRIPTIONS,

BEAUTIFUL PLEASURE GROUNDS, PLANTATIONS, GARDENS,

FINE STREAM OF WATER,

Entrance Lodges,

FARM, AND LAND,

CONTAINING

TWO HUNDRED AND THIRTY ACR

OR THEREABOUTS,

CALLED

WALL HALL,

SITUATE IN A FINE HEALTHY AND BEAUTIFUL PART OF THE COUNTY OF H

Three Miles from Watford, Five from St. Albans, and Sixteen from London,

PARTLY SITUATE IN THE PARISHES OF ALDENHAM AND SAINT STEPHEN,

And partly Extra-Parochial,

A MOST DESIRABLE PROPERTY FOR A GENTLEMA

And fit for immediate Occupation :

WHICH WILL BE SOLD BY AUCTION,

BY MR. ROBINS,

At Garraway's Coffee-House, Change-Alley, Cornhill,

LONDON,

On THURSDAY, the 28th of MAY, 1812, at TWELVE O'CLOCK, in ONE

BY ORDER OF THE TRUSTEES OF THE LATE MR. THELLUSSON.

To be viewed by Tickets, and by applying to Mr. Thomas Smith, the Bailiff, at Wall Hall, where Particulars ma
at the Essex Arms, Watford; Red Lion, Elstree; White Hart, Edgware; Abercorn Arms, Stanmore; W
St. Albans; Bell, Hertford; of Messrs. Oddie, Oddie, and Forster, Solicitors, Carey-Street, Lincoln's-Inn;
Architect, Gower-Street, Bedford-Square; at Garraway's; and of Mr. ROBINS, Warwick-Street, Golden-Squa
Tickets for Viewing may be had, and a Plan of the Estate seen.

ABOVE: Admiral Sir Charles Maurice Pole, bought CENTRE: Wall Hall (ERB) in 1812 and lived there until
his death in 1831. (NMM) BELOW: William Stuart bought the house from Sir Maurice Pole's widow in 1842
and lived there until his death in 1874. RIGHT: Particulars of the sale of Wall Hall mansion and part of the estate
following the death of George Woodford Thellusson in 1811. (HCRO)

John Pierpont Morgan bought the house (through his wife) from the Stuart family in 1910. A Royal shooting party at Wall Hall in 1938. Pierpont Morgan is standing in the middle of the back row: on his right is King George VI and in front of him sits Queen Elizabeth. (HCRO)

ABOVE: Wall Hall: the front entrance; the portico was added by William Stuart in the 1840s. BELOW: Munden, c1900: the earliest part of the house dates from about 1720, but most of the present 'Gothic' mansion dates from the early 19th century. OPPOSITE ABOVE LEFT: Munden, seen from the River Colne, c1900. RIGHT: Otterspool House, by the River Colne, c1910. This 18th century house was originally a hotel and the centre of a small spa, where the waters of the pool were drunk. Converted to a private house early in the 19th century for the widow of George Woodford Thellusson after the sale of Wall Hall in 1812, it is now a hostel for students at the college. CENTRE LEFT: Otterspool Bridge, spanning the River Colne which (apart from an enclave taking in Munden on the far bank) has formed the northern boundary of Aldenham for more than a thousand years. RIGHT: Kendal's Hall, c1910 was the home of successive generations of the Phillimore family until 1926. It now houses the Radlett Preparatory School. BELOW: Piggott's Manor, Letchmore Heath was rebuilt in 1884 in mock-Tudor style, on the site of earlier buildings extending back to the 12th century. Purchased in 1973 by George Harrison for use by the International Society for Krishna Consciousness as a theological training college, it is now renamed Bhaktivedanta Manor. (RCHM)

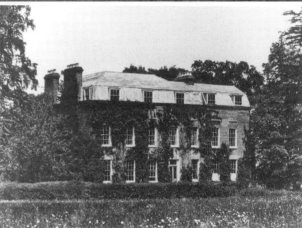

ABOVE: Aldenham Church and former vicarage, from the east. The Georgian vicarage was substantially remodelled and given a new front with a dentil cornice in the 1890s by Archdeacon Gibbs. A new vicarage was built close by in the 1960s and the original building, renamed Glebe House, is now divided into two dwellings. BELOW: Aldenham Church of St John the Baptist, southern aspect. The spire was destroyed by enemy bombs in the Second World War and has been replaced with the present rather taller one.

Aldenham: Heart of the Parish

The dispersed pattern of early settlement in the Parish created by the nature of the environment — mainly woodland, in which 'breaks', 'breaches' or clearings were constantly being made — and the generally small tenancies administered by the Abbots of Westminster, persisted until the dissolution of the monasteries. Apart from a small cluster of houses around the Church there were no nucleated settlements.

With the changed pattern of land-holding that emerged after the sixteenth century, and progressive enclosure of common lands, the dispossessed tenants and other farm labourers as well as a growing number of tradesmen tended to group together in communities or hamlets, of which about a dozen can be identified within the Parish. Initially, the chief among these was Aldenham hamlet itself, the Church and the manor house providing a natural focus.

It is a curious quirk of social evolution that the community of Aldenham, despite its long history and its central position on medieval routeways, as well as its early status as the administrative and social centre of the Parish, has never developed into anything more than a small village. The earliest primitive dwelling houses were sited around a pond, now in the grounds of Edge Grove School, before the construction of the Church led to a shift in the centre of the settlement. There is mention in the seventeenth century of a 'Church House', a 'Kitchen House' and a 'Clerk's House', which stood together close to the Church and were then in a ruinous condition. Sir Edward Cary, the lord of the manor, arranged an exchange of land at Priest's Heath near Berry Grove for the sites of these three houses, so that he could round off his park at this point. There was also a second 'Church House', which stood opposite the Church, approximately on the site where the former Chequers Inn, now the Aldenham Social Club, was built about the year 1631; parts of the old building may have been incorporated in it. An early farmhouse, originally called Place Farm and more recently Church Farm, also stands near the Church and site of Aldenham Place; within the present building there is a tiebeam inscribed 1689 though the front is from the early eighteenth century.

In 1641, Lord Falkland sold some of the land in and around Aldenham to Edward Bowes and his daughter. The indenture of the sale included 'the house of John Downer called the Church House, otherwise commonly called by the name of Smoakey House' as well as the 'New Inn', a quite separate establishment first referred to in an earlier indenture of 1621 and probably located near Kemp Row on the Oakridge Lane route to St Albans. The Bowes family are thought to have lived in the New Inn until John Skey, who married into the family, built himself a mansion at Edge Grove on or close to the site about the year 1725.

Yet another inn, the Compasses, about which even less is known, was situated on the old Jackets Lane (which disappeared following the enclosures of 1803), by the Edge Grove pond; and it may be that this inn, the 'Smoakey House' and the New Inn were all serving the alcoholic needs of the small population of Aldenham at one and the same time, their tenants probably ekeing out a living by farming smallholdings. The Compasses is said to have disappeared about the time when George Woodford Thellusson built Wall Hall in 1803. The old cottages around the pond were also demolished around then, their inmates probably finding refuge in the Aldenham workhouse.

The workhouse was undoubtedly the most significant feature of life in Aldenham village during the eighteenth and early nineteenth centuries. It was in 1725 that an Act of Parliament first enabled parishes to combine for the purpose of creating a workhouse, thereby giving rise to the term 'union' as a euphemism for the dreaded institution, and soon afterwards a small workhouse was built in Aldenham immediately adjoining the Chequers Inn. This was superseded by a larger building erected on part of the yard and garden belonging to the old one, which remained in use until the new Poor Law of 1834 created further unions, as part of which Aldenham was merged into the Watford Union. The original workhouse had been converted into three cottages, which remained the property of the Parish until they were pulled down in 1923.

Much has been written about living conditions and the social environment in the English workhouse system; no doubt Aldenham was typical. Few detailed records have survived, but an inventory taken in 1791 and now in the County Record Office gives some idea of the starkness of the environment, as the listing of the contents of a couple of the rooms show:

'Women's room adjoining the men's: three sacking bottom bedsteads; one other bedstead; four feather beds; four bolsters; five blankets; four cover lids; one chest of drawers; one oak chest; two deal boxes; two chairs and two stools.

'Little room called the parlour: one deal table top and form; a round wainscot table; one rush bottom chair; one pair bellows; one fire shovel, two pairs of tongs, one poker; one fender, an hanging iron and trivet; a pair of steelyards and a brass ladle; one copper drinking set; two cullenders; a blower and flat irons, six stone plates, eighteen trenchers, six wooden dishes; and a dudgeon [knife] box.'

When the workhouse was closed in 1835 the premises were acquired by the then owner of Wall Hall, William Stuart, and converted into a superior inn with large lock-up coach houses, good stabling and a brewhouse; it was intended to attract hunting men. It was called the Red Lion Inn and its first landlord was a member of the local Burnell family; he was succeeded by a William Saunders. However, the inn was not a success and was closed down in 1845, when the building was converted into a terrace of nine cottages, each let for a rent not exceeding £4 a year. The building today stands as a terrace of four cottages, still known as the Red Lion Cottages. The licence of the Red Lion Inn was moved to premises newly built at the corner of Hilfield Lane, and in 1959 it was again transferred to a commodious new building on the Watford Bypass at Cox's Corner; some years ago the traditional name was replaced by the more equivocal appellation of The Game Bird.

Throughout the nineteenth century Aldenham remained a quiet village where nothing much happened. The abandoning of the manor house early in the eighteenth century; the remoteness of many of the lords of the manor, and the disinclination of the owners of Wall Hall to take much interest in local affairs left something of a vacuum so far as patronage was concerned. The first census of 1841 lists a bare dozen households in the community: by 1881 this had only risen to 22, of which eleven were living in the original workhouse buildings, mostly agricultural labourers employed at local farms.

The 1881 census shows only two householders of substance. Church Farm was occupied by Richard Hedges, a bachelor of 30, recorded as farming 360 acres and employing 12 men and four boys; the farmhouse was shared with his unmarried sister, Mary, and one living-in domestic servant aged 16. By contrast the adjacent vicarage housed 13 people: the vicar, Charles Royd, and his wife Catherine; an unmarried son and daughter; a married son, his wife and their eight-month-old son, and six living-in servants described variously as cook, kitchen maid, parlour maid, domestic nurse, ladies' maid and housemaid. The vicar's coachman and family occupied the stable block built in an old quarry in the garden (now a private house called The Dell).

The vicarage itself reflected the standing of the vicar: a handsome Georgian red brick house of five bays, which was substantially remodelled and given a new front by Royd's successor, Archdeacon Kenneth Gibbs (son of the first Lord Aldenham), in the 1890s. Since the last war a new and rather more manageable vicarage has been provided for the incumbent; the Georgian building still stands, but has been converted into two separate residences now known as Glebe House.

Much of the Church of St John the Baptist has remained unchanged since the fourteenth century, when the nave and south side were built, and the fifteenth century, when the north side was added. In 1813 a restoration was undertaken in response to an order from Archdeacon Middleton of Huntingdon, who found it 'much out of repair, several parts of the church being in a state of dilapidation and decay'. The following year the spire, then covered with lead weighing two and a half tons, was reportedly dangerous. Parishioners wanted it removed, thinking that the tower would 'look full well without it', but they were restrained by the Archdeacon and it was rebuilt, using oak shingles. In 1843 the musicians' gallery under the tower, and the Aldenham School gallery erected by the Brewers Company in 1686, were removed.

The fortunes of the Church were enhanced when the vicarage and advowson were sold in 1877 by the then lord of the manor to Henry Hucks Gibbs of Aldenham House. Gibbs undertook a thorough restoration in 1882 and provided new furnishings at the considerable cost for those days of £11,000, employing distinguished architect Sir Arthur Blomfield. Twenty years later, as Lord Aldenham, he financed further improvements, including the provision of a new chancel screen designed by C.J. Blomfield.

On 16 October 1940 the Church was severely damaged by a stray stick of German bombs. The spire was demolished and in falling caused substantial further damage; most of the windows were also broken. Further bombs fell in the churchyard, breaking many headstones and disturbing several graves. Between the end of the war and 1973 a further comprehensive restoration was carried out and, despite further representations against it, the spire was once again replaced, an extra eighteen inches being added to its height in order to give a better proportion to the tower. A new church room and choir vestry were added in 1970 in commemoration of the 700th anniversary; the first additions to the building since the seventeenth century.

Although changes have been made over the centuries without any regard to symmetry or consistency, Canon Bill Ritson (who was vicar between 1976 and 1987) sums the Church up in the following terms: 'The building is the more interesting, and perhaps more beautiful, because the additions and alterations through the centuries are so unsymmetrical. No one seems to have troubled to make the new match the old. There is a broad aisle on the north side and a narrow aisle on the south side; the chancel arch is far out of centre; the west door is not opposite the altar; on the south side there are three arches, while on the north there is a much later arch and half an arch; the window over the north door is not centred with it; and yet the whole building is very pleasing'.

It was not until the present century that Aldenham village received any real local patronage. The Wall Hall estate acquired by the banker J. Pierpont Morgan in 1912 was managed purposefully for perhaps the first time in its existence. One of Morgan's shrewd — if, as a financier, perhaps not entirely altruistic — decisions was to ensure that workers on the estate were provided with adequate local housing. To this end, he arranged for a number of houses to be built on estate land in the village near the main gateway to Wall Hall. Most of these were constructed along an access road known as The Crescent around the southern and western sides of the village green; two more pairs in matching vernacular style are known as Dairy Cottages and Church Farm Cottages. When the Wall Hall estate was acquired by Hertfordshire County Council in 1942 these houses were taken over as Council properties for letting: in recent years they have been sold off.

Morgan was also instrumental in renovating Church Farm and its outbuildings to turn it into a 'model' farm. Currently the future of the whole of the now redundant Church Farm is under review, to ensure that this site in the very heart of Aldenham remains an attractive feature of the conservation village.

Round Bush, High Cross and Kemp Row

Slightly detached from Aldenham but historically associated with it are the hamlets of Round Bush, High Cross and Kemp Row. This area largely evolved after the enclosures of 1803, which caused the road system to be altered so as to give more privacy to the occupants of Edge Grove House. Although Round Bush is shown as such on Camden's map of 1607, and the first reference in the parish registers dates from 1642, at the start of the nineteenth century there was only one house standing — which still survives, now called Corner Cottage — occupied by Thomas Hadnutt, a leaseholder whose forbears had farmed in the district for well over two centuries. The name is traditionally ascribed to an old, round, holly bush, which used to stand near Corner Cottage.

The enclosures resulted in the Round Bush triangle of roads being built and, after Hadnutt disposed of his interest, the land was acquired by Sir Charles Pole of Aldenham Abbey (Wall Hall). Development of the area started in 1826 with the building of a National School, the first free school for children of the Parish, and in 1839 the then owners of Aldenham Abbey put up four almshouses (since rebuilt). Two ale houses followed, the Volunteer and the Round Bush; the former later closed down and the latter in due course acquired a full licence. A former blacksmith's premises, now the garage, was erected in 1840. There was also a grocer's shop and an early police station for horse patrols. By 1841 the hamlet had achieved virtually its present-day size, with 22 dwellings and a population of 82.

High Cross, so-called because it stands at the highest point of the area where four pre-enclosure roads met, developed over about the same period as Round Bush and in 1841 had eleven dwellings with 48 inhabitants. Early on, a bakery was established near the entrance to Edge Grove, run by William Holloway who, with the assistance of two baker journeymen, was probably the first person in the Parish to bake bread on a large scale, as well as to offer the use of his ovens for the cooking of meals. The bakehouse closed in 1896 when Henry Cole, the then proprietor, moved to new premises in Radlett.

The earliest reference to Edge Grove appears in 1236 when the Abbot of Westminster granted one acre of land near 'Hemhegge Grove' to Symon, chaplain of Aldenham village; subsequently a number of cottages were established around the fish pond (now a lake), near the old road from High Cross to Aldenham. Most of the cottages were pulled down early in the eighteenth century, when John Skey bought the property and built the central part of the present house. In about 1800 it was acquired by Sir John Nicholl of Doctors Commons in London, who expanded the estate before selling out to the Thellusson trustees of Wall Hall, the house being occupied throughout this time by a number of tenants. One of these was Charles Edward Barnett, who greatly enlarged the premises and improved the grounds in the late nineteenth century; his daughter married Archdeacon Gibbs, vicar of Aldenham. The mansion, as it had now become, was acquired with the rest of the Wall Hall estate in 1910 by Pierpont Morgan, and in 1935 it was leased to Captain Pratt and Mr Waterfield, who started up the preparatory school for boys which has since grown and flourished.

Kemp Row, where the monasterial gallows stood on the main route from Aldenham to St Albans, was little more than the site of a farmhouse until recent times. John Charrington, son of a vicar of Aldenham and founder of Charrington's Brewery, owned the farm prior to his death in 1815, but let it to tenants. The present house, dating from the early nineteenth century, is now a listed building. The Nook, a cottage opposite the farm, is a single-storey building dating from about 1500; the two-storeyed front was added about 1600.

LEFT: Church Farm, Aldenham — a timber-framed house dating from the 16th century, with a further bay bearing the date 1682 carved on a tiebeam. An additional brick range facing the road was added in the 18th century with symmetrical facade and mansard roof. Acquired by Pierpont Morgan as the nucleus of a model farm and dairy it is now owned by Hertfordshire County Council. (RCHM)

T: The Chequers Inn, Aldenham, c1913: a timber-framed hall built about 1630 (though the present front is early 18th century) robably an alehouse all its life, it was acquired by Pierpont n in the 1920s and delicensed by him in the interests of rance; it now houses the Aldenham Social Club. BELOW: The stable range of Aldenham vicarage, now a private residence called The Dell.

ABOVE: Red Lion Cottages, Aldenham; built in the late 18th century as the parish workhouse, the building later had a short and unsuccessful life as a superior inn called the Red Lion, intended to attract hunting men. It was converted to a terrace of nine cottages in 1845, and now forms four dwellings. BELOW: The green at Aldenham; the houses forming a crescent around it were built by Pierpont Morgan for workers on the Wall Hall Estate. OPPOSITE: Decorations erected in Aldenham to celebrate the wedding of the vicar, Archdeacon Kenneth Gibbs, in the 1890s. (HCRO)

ABOVE: The Aldenham church choir in 1911. Archdeacon Kenneth Gibbs is in the centre, on his right the curate, Mr Finch, and on his left the organist, Miss Boff. BELOW: The central part of Edge Grove House was built in the early 18th century by John Skey and greatly enlarged in the late 19th century. Since 1935 it has housed a preparatory school for boys. (RCHM)

ABOVE: Children's fancy dress party at the Aldenham Social Club, 1929.
BELOW: Ivy Cottages, Aldenham, in 1903; they were built c1800 as estate
cottages for the new mansion of Aldenham Abbey (Wall Hall). In the
photograph are members of the Jeffery and Simpson families, who occupied
two of the cottages. The baby on William Simpson's shoulder, now Mrs
Marsh, still lives there.

ABOVE: Round Bush, c1900; the almshouses were built by the
Stuarts of Wall Hall in the 1850s, and demolished in the 1920s
when the present cottages were erected. CENTRE: Delrow
Almshouses, c1905, erected by the Brewers Company in 1865.
BELOW: Delrow School, c1905, built to replace the old Lower
School at Aldenham.

Letchmore Heath: An English Village

A mile or so to the south-east of Aldenham village lies what became the most considerable settlement in the Parish until the start of the present century. Its name, first recorded in 1299 as Lachmeres Heth, comes from Anglo-Saxon words meaning 'muddy pond heath'; by the sixteenth century it had evolved into the near-modern Lechmore Heath. In Saxon times, what later became known as the Great Common of Aldenham was mainly a forest but, over the centuries, the settlers cleared the northern half, leaving the area to the south of Letchmore Heath as woodland until after the monastic period. Early Parish rate books refer to the areas north and south of the village as 'Fieldside' and 'Woodside', while the early Sawyer's Lane, which ran from old Grubb's Lane northwards and in places was sixty feet wide, suggests a thoroughfare along which timber was carried on its way to London.

On the edge of the cleared area, the village grew up at the gates of Piggott's Manor. Although theirs was never a true manor in the administrative sense, the lords of Piggotts enjoyed almost as much authority as those of Aldenham and Titberst & Kendals, and many of the early villagers were in their employ. Some local industry developed, principally concerned with cloth manufacture, and may go as far back as the reign of Charles I. An old factory was in operation locally at the end of the eighteenth century (hence 'Factory field' for the land opposite), which was encouraged by the Hon George Villiers, owner of nearby Hilfield Castle. In 1821 it was rebuilt by a Major Geary for straw plaiting and hat manufacture. The 1851 census lists eleven females in Letchmore Heath whose occupation was straw hat manufacture, but none appears in the 1861 census, which suggests that by then the industry had wound up in the face of competition from new production centres in Luton and Dunstable.

There must have been enough people in the late Tudor period to encourage Richard Platt, a London businessman and brewer who owned lands in the vicinity, to establish a grammar school in 1599 to the south of the village on Boyden's Hill. Platt's 'good and charitable Intent and Purpose' seems more idealistic than realistic, for a more out-of-the-way site for a grammar school — presumably intended to compare with other such schools — can scarcely be imagined. Platt died soon after Aldenham School opened and his bequests were subsequently administered by the City of London Brewers Company; it was merciful that he did not live long enough to witness the rapid and sad decline of the school, which led a pitiful hand-to-mouth existence for the next two centuries.

The Court Books of the Brewers Company are full of stark references to negligences, incompetencies and misdemeanours of an ever-changing string of masters and tutors. Much of this was no doubt due to the low income from the trust fund and the consequently low salaries awarded by the Company. In 1672, a report on the 'badness of the free school by reason of the fewness of Schollers and the non-proficiency of those that are there' led to a plan to close the school and spend the 'overplus' of the Platt Estate on a Free School at Watford, a proposal which was received as 'a great kindness' by the inhabitants of that town. However, the objection of the then lord of the manor to having Aldenham money spent on Watford led to abandonment, and the school survived.

Despite occasional reports of improvements thereafter, the story on the whole remained one of low registers (an average of 35–40 scholars), absentee masters in financial difficulties, and an almost total lack of instruction. A nadir was reached in the 1790s when one report of the Visitors spoke of the school being in the worst condition they could ever remember, and another recorded that there were only 24 pupils of whom very few could read.

In 1818 the Charity Commissioners investigated the Platt Trust Fund and the condition of the school. Their scathing public report coincided with a substantial increase in the income of the Trust; the Brewers Company decided to improve the school. By 1825 they had built a new Lower School for 60 to 80 boys and appointed a master with a salary of £60 a year to teach them reading, writing and arithmetic. They then pulled down the old Elizabethan school building, which had become too ruinous to repair, and built a new school for the reception of 50 boarders, sons of freemen of the Company or inhabitants of Aldenham. Of these two schools, the Lower School did good work for the next 35 years, a large number of boys getting a solid, basic education until the building fell out of repair and was replaced by two elementary schools for boys at Medburn and Delrow, financed by the Platt Estates.

The boarding school was certainly not as useful during that same period, with only about ten scholarship boys a year up to 1850, plus ten to fifteen private pupils. At all events, a real classical and mathematical education was given to the few boys who were there, and in 1858 a scholar 'obtained the high degree of 6th Wrangler'. In that year the Charity Commissioners again took an interest. Following a voluminous report, a new scheme for the management of the Platt Estate was launched, leading to some improvements. These were, however, largely nullified by the obstruction and general antipathy of the longstanding headmaster, Rev Alfred Leeman. It was not until 1876, when Mr Leeman was induced to retire after more than thirty years in charge, with what passed in those days for a golden handshake, that the turning point came with the appointment of Rev John Kennedy. Thereafter, Aldenham School never looked back, and expansion in staff, scholars and facilities was rapid.

Kennedy was persuaded to stay for the rest of his career, despite offers elsewhere and, when he resigned at Christmas 1899 after 23 years' service, Kenneth Gibbs, vicar of Aldenham, wrote as follows: 'The best day's work that was ever done for Aldenham School was done on July 17th 1876, when Mr Kennedy was elected to the Headmastership. It is impossible to over-estimate what the School owes to him, he had a difficult job to do and he did it through 23 years with unbroken and most remarkable success. He found the School small and disorderly and he left it nearly four times as large as he found it and with a reputation for character and for education of which any School might be proud'.

Kennedy's successors have carried on his excellent work and in the present century Aldenham School has risen to a distinguished status among the country's small public schools. Its estate comprises 135 acres of grounds and farmland, and its complex of buildings include some fine modern examples, notably the Stott Library (housing a collection of around 25,000 books plus other research material), and the chapel.

At the same time as he founded the school, Richard Platt built six almshouses adjacent to it 'for the relief of the Poor decayed and ympotent P'sons', the maintenance of which was due to be financed from the rent of a house in Knight Ryder Street, London which he left to the Brewers Company in his will. Again, the Court Books of the Company tell some tales of woe and mismanagement, and in 1661 it is recorded that the almspeople were to be suspended for pawning their gowns. When the major reconstruction of the School took place in the 1860s, new almshouses were built at Delrow adjacent to the new boys' school, also financed by the Platt Trust, and the old ones were pulled down.

Back in the village of Letchmore Heath, life came to be centred mainly around the Three Horseshoes Inn, facing the village green, which has traded as a beerhouse since at least the eighteenth century, possibly earlier. The house is recorded in a survey of 1586 together with an adjoining smith's shop, which remained a working smithy until recent times. The earliest part of the building is a timber-framed hall dating from the sixteenth century. The attractive frontage is mainly from the seventeenth or eighteenth century, but the building was substantially reconstructed, both as a public house and a smithy, in about 1803. The building, and indeed the whole village, has featured in many film settings since the 1920s, following the growth of the industry at nearby Boreham Wood.

Another inn in the village was the Bricklayers' Arms, built about 1810 at the corner of Common Lane and Elstree Road and operating as a beerhouse by 1841. Its name came from the first tenant, John Childs, a bricklayer. Universally known to local inhabitants as 'The Brick', it was destroyed in an air raid during the Second World War, killing the landlady and a small girl, by a bomb from the same stick that also damaged Aldenham Church.

Throughout the nineteenth century, Letchmore Heath remained the hub of the Parish. By the 1830s, a post office had already been established there in a building which still stands, though now a private house: The Old Rest, reputedly the oldest house in the village. It was run by William Moth, also listed in the trade directory as a grocer and a tailor (and who, in such spare time as he had, also farmed six acres of land). Carpenters, bricklayers, baker, mealman, blacksmith, higgler (itinerant dealer) and (as a link with the outside world) a carrier, provided a high degree of self-sufficiency in meeting the simple needs of the predominantly agricultural population. In 1851, there were 51 agricultural labourers living in the village.

After the death of William Moth, the village store was carried on for many years by his widow, Mary. A former pupil of Aldenham School records in his memoirs: 'For tuck of all kinds we resorted to Mother Moth (what a delightful Shakespearian name!); I do not remember that the stock of eatables was either large or varied. The one thing that is strongly imprinted on my mind is the great Saturday afternoon feast of hot sausages flavoured with vinegar in which you indulged if you had sufficient pocket money left at the end of the week, or if you could persuade Mother Moth to let you have tick'.

Another former schoolboy recalls: 'My first acquaintance with sloe gin was gained at Aldenham made from gathered sloes, looted sugar (provided from the matron's larder, we'll be bound) and gin from the "Three Horseshoes" . . . I can remember a noble pike, weight about 14 lbs, from the Munden water near Watford which, baked in a village oven at old Mary Moth's tuck-shop, helped to tame a real tightener for four hungry boys. On pig-killing days in the village we used to buy excellent pork sausages for 6d a lb, and have loaves of new bread on baking days'.

Even as late as the 1920s, the village remained largely self-sufficient for everyday living. The Old Rest continued as a general store, and there were two other grocers, at No 1 Leaper Cottages and Palfreys, a bakery and a newsagent and confectioners. The separate post office also housed a tailor, and another one operated from Sunnyside. A greengrocer was at No 1 Common Lane, and Offley Cottage sold haberdashery. Local tradesmen were abundant and one builder doubled as an undertaker. The smithy still operated from his shop next to the Three Horseshoes.

Most of the Victorian houses had been built by members of the Burnell family, who had settled there by the 1830s, and several generations traded as building craftsmen. Ronald Burnell, the last surviving local member of the family, recalls that timber for the houses was felled, seasoned and then processed by his great-grandfather, grandfather and great uncles in a sawyer's pit close to the Three Horseshoes. The Memorial Hall was built in 1920 by public subscription to commemorate the fallen of World War One. Mr Burnell remembers that most of the village assisted in its construction, his own contribution as a small boy being to dig the clay and puddle the bricks.

One twentieth century building of note is the neo-Georgian Aldenham Grange, designed by Walter Cave and built around 1910 for Mr K.W. Edgcumbe, a successful electrical engineer and owner of Everett Edgcumbe & Co of Hendon who, relatively late in life at the age of 70, and somewhat to his surprise, became the Sixth Earl of Mount Edgcumbe, when his cousin, the fifth Earl, died without an heir. The new Lord Mount Edgcumbe, who by that time had moved from Letchmore Heath, thereafter lived mainly at the family seat of Cotehele in Cornwall (now a notable property of the National Trust) until his death in 1944 in his ninety-second year.

By the 1950s, the number of shops had dwindled to three. Elizabeth Robertson remembers: 'In my youth there was The Old Rest which was the most intriguing shop for a young girl. It was always packed full of goodies, my best memory being of the rows of large glass jars of sweets behind the counter. Mrs Carlisle, who owned the shop then, always put our sweets in cones which she made from squares of paper. They were marvellous, because invariably when you thought you had eaten all your sweets there would be one hiding right down at the bottom of the cone. She also had an enormous ham slicer at the back of the shop which made a lovely swishing noise. I was sometimes allowed into the back to watch her slicing the meat: it was a great treat. Even though it was a tiny shop she seemed to sell everything possible, one didn't need to go anywhere else for provisions.

'The other amazing shop was Daisy Green's General Stores and, although selling the same kind of things as The Old Rest it was an experience never to miss. I can't really remember very much about this shop, as it closed down when I was quite young, but I do remember Daisy Green herself. She was a marvellous old dear, but to find her in the shop was like looking for a needle in a haystack and once you had found her you had to wait for ages until she found what you wanted. She would scutter away and, eventually, if you were lucky, come back with it. I can still remember the dusty, creaky floorboards and the musty smell that surrounded you when you walked in. There was a huge counter which looked as though it had been there for centuries, and piled high on top were stacks of tin boxes with trade names such as 'Cadbury' and 'Frys' written in gold on the front. This shop closed down when Daisy herself died, as it was a family business and she had no one to take over from her. For years afterwards the shop stayed unchanged but empty, the old 'Brooke Bond' signs on the window.

'The third shop, and the only one that still exists now, was purely a newsagents when I was young. There only used to be a tiny counter just inside the door where everyone collected their papers but, as the other shops closed down, the newsagents was extended to serve as the general stores and post office for the whole village.'

Today, even this general stores has gone; its most recent commercial use was as a health food shop of the local Krishna community.

Letchmore Heath, before the motor car came, had always been a workaday village of labourers and artisans, and the dwellings in it generally modest. Some of the surviving timber-framed cottages from the sixteenth and seventeenth century such as Apple Tree, Rose and Jasmine Cottages, The Old Rest and Piggotts Manor Cottage now have great period charm and are rightly preserved as listed buildings, together with the more imposing eighteenth century villa in Common Lane known as The Fortress (which has the interesting feature of a rear turret incorporating an ornamental lighthouse with stained glass facets). But the occupants of the present day are markedly different in type from those of former years, since the attractions of a picture-postcard village, complete with traditional green and pond, yet so close to main roads and London, now make it one of the most desirable living places in the London hinterland.

Aldenham Wood

South of Letchmore Heath there used to be the ancient medieval hamlet of Aldenham Wood, at road junctions where the old Grubbs Lane and Hog Lane met the Elstree Road. The first recorded reference was in 1382 and there is some evidence that a chapel was established there prior to the dissolution of the monasteries, near the large houses of Wigbournes and Penne's Place, its building surviving into Elizabethan times, when it was used as a meeting place. In 1851 some 81 people lived in the hamlet, which included Dagger Farm (later known as Queensbury Lodge), Page's Farm and the Wrestlers Inn. This public house seemingly derived its name from its use as a training ground for pugilists.

At the end of the nineteenth century the hamlet virtually disappeared, when the newly-ennobled Henry Hucks Gibbs enclosed much of its territory as part of the parkland of Aldenham House and demolished most of the houses. He diverted the Elstree Road, which used to run close to the mansion, further west and closed Grubbs Lane. In place of the latter he built a new lane about 250 metres to the north, at the boundary of the enlarged park, which was at first called New Grubbs Lane but later — the locals saying that it had emerged from its chrysalis — this was changed to the more attractive Butterfly Lane. The old line of the Elstree Road is marked by cottages which still survive either side of Butterfly Lane. Lord Aldenham also demolished the Wrestlers Inn and built in its place, at the new road junction, the present Battleaxes Inn (the name taken from a motif on the Aldenham coat of arms). As part of this enclosure the site of the thirteenth century Penne's Place was also absorbed within the park. Much of the land formerly belonging to Page's Farm is now taken up by Elstree aerodrome (which actually lies within Aldenham Parish).

Three Horseshoes, Letchmore Heath, drawn by Ted Barker.

ABOVE: Aldenham School in 1825, and BELOW: in 1907 — Mr Beevor's
House. OPPOSITE ABOVE: The School in 1907. BELOW: Old houses in
Letchmore Heath, 1890.

ABOVE: The Green, Letchmore Heath c1900, and BELOW: Back Lane,
Letchmore Heath c1905.

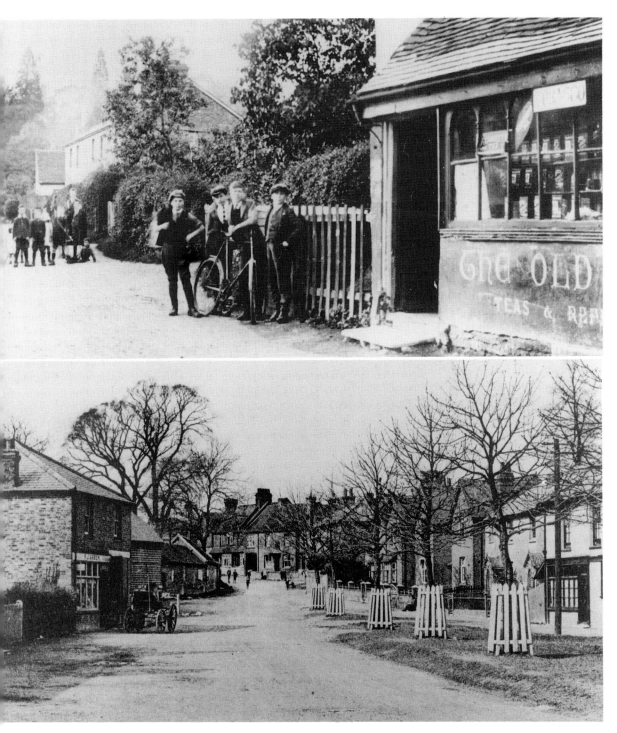

ABOVE: Back Lane, with The Old Rest on the right, and BELOW: the
village centre, Letchmore Heath c1910.

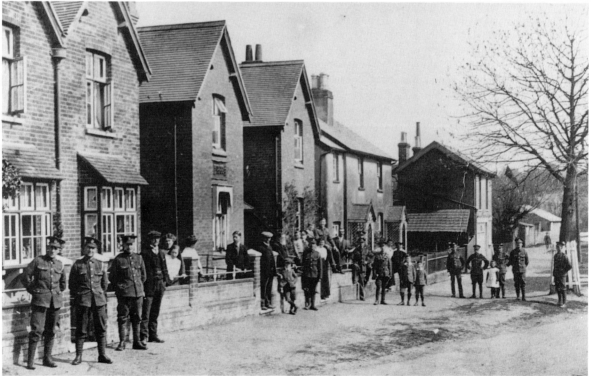

ABOVE: The village about 1910. BELOW: Troops billeted at Letchmore
Heath in 1915.

ABOVE: Letchmore Heath in 1935. (FHS) BELOW: The Three Horseshoes
public house in the 1920s.

ABOVE: The old smithy, Letchmore Heath, c1900. BELOW: Unveiling the
war memorial, Letchmore Heath.

LEFT: The Memorial Hall and post office, Letchmore Heath, in the 1920s.
RIGHT: The Bricklayers Arms public house, destroyed by enemy action
1941. BELOW: The Aldenham Harriers passing the bombed remains of the
Bricklayers Arms.

ABOVE: The Wrestlers public house, Aldenham Wood, demolished by Lord Aldenham in the 1890s when the land was added to his estate. (LA) BELOW: Aldenham Reservoir in the 1930s. (FHS)

Radlett: A Sweet Retired Spot

The name of Radlett (usually spelled with one 't' until the mid-nineteenth century) appears to have evolved from the Old-English *rad-gelaete* meaning a junction of roads, and it is clear that the settlement grew at the point where the ancient route from Aldenham to Shenley crosses Watling Street. The first recorded reference to 'Radelet' comes from 1453, but it is quite possible that some dwellings existed much earlier. The first entry in parish registers comes in 1560, recording the christening of 'Edward Warner, ye sonne of Jo Wa. (of Radlet)'. The Warners were yeomen who farmed in a number of places in the neighbourhood for over two centuries and then disappeared.

Few references appear in the registers over the succeeding centuries, and Radlett seems to have consisted of two farms, one large (Darnhills) and one small (Gills Hill) on the west side of Watling Street, and the estates of Aldenham Lodge, Newberries and Organ Hall on the east, plus Newlands and a few cottages. At least one of the two inns at the cross-roads, the Cross Keys (now The Railway public house) and the Red Lion, must have existed for a long time, but there are no firm records concerning either before the end of the eighteenth century.

Despite its antiquity, not much through traffic used the stretch of Watling Street between Elstree and St Albans, which had degenerated to little more than a muddy track. In coaching days, Radlett became effectively bypassed to the east by Telford's new Holyhead Road, which carried travellers from London to St Albans *via* Barnet, and to the west by the turnpike road running from the Edgware Road *via* Stanmore and Watford.

In J. Hassall's *Rides & Walks with Excursions by Water Thirty Miles round the British Metropolis, 1817* there appears this reference to the Cross Keys:
'Aldenham stands near Watling Street, is a sweet retired spot with an abundance of noble timber in its neighbourhood and generally abounding with game. The best headquarters for shooting in this neighbourhood will be found at the "Cross Keys" at the village of Radlet, situate on the high road from Elstree to St Albans'.

Until the 1860s there was a smithy at the rear of the Cross Keys, and a livery stables which did not vanish until the late 1920s, and it was here that in pre-railway days a traveller on one of the few coaches passing through Radlett could hire a horse or a chaise. The tenant of the inn in the 1830s and '40s was William Hadnutt, a member of a family which had lived and farmed in the Parish for some centuries.

The old Red Lion was owned throughout the nineteenth century by just two families: first the Clarks (over three generations) and then the Wings, who were in possession until it was demolished in 1905. The smithy at the Cross Keys was transferred to the other inn when Tom Wing acquired it, but his son, James, soon set up a separate blacksmith's shop in the yard of the detached flint house across the road, next to the Flint Cottages (which had themselves been built by the Phillimore family in 1852 to replace a mass of derelict earlier cottages known derogatorily as 'The Barracks'). His principal employee was William Andrews, who took over the business in the 1880s and built it into a flourishing concern employing seven men.

The Flint Cottages, drawn by Ted Barker.

Darnhills has a history which goes back well over six centuries. In 1358 John de Dernewell, who probably gave his name to the estate, was a witness to a document transferring lands of the Manor of Titberst. In his will dated 20 August 1423, his son, John Dernewell, left lands at Aldenham and bequeathed money to the Church; he was undoubtedly the owner of the messuage and lands called Dernewells or Darnells, and later Darnhills. His property descended through his daughter, Margaret, to her son, John Penne, a member of the family living at Penne's Place. From him it apparently passed just as Penne's Place did, for in 1671 Dernewells was granted by Henry Coghill of Wigbournes to John, his son. A farm called Darnells, shown on Dury & Andrews' map of 1766, belonged to Sarah Coghill, who married Robert Hucks and willed the property to their son, Robert. In the 1830s it consisted of some 184 acres and had passed into the possession of William Robert Phillimore, who let it out to tenants. Darnhills farm continued to flourish until the early part of this century but it gradually faded out when the land was progressively given over to housing development. The Darnhills house itself, mentioned in John Norden's survey of the early seventeenth century, was finally demolished around 1970, when the present block of flats bearing the name was built. The narrow Malt Lane, which for many years formed the northern boundary of the Parish, is thought to have derived its name from a small maltings within the complex of the Darnhill's estate.

Newlands is also shown on Dury & Andrews' map and has an even older recorded history than Darnhills. This small estate, which until recent times was in the Parish of St Stephens, was in the possession of the Abbot of St Albans. The first reference under the name of Neweland comes in 1291; later monasterial records refer to it in Latin as *Nova Terra*. The name would have related to a patch of original woodland which had been cleared for cultivation. After the dissolution it was granted to Sir Richard Lee of Sopwell; later it descended to his daughter Mary's second husband, Sir Humphrey Coningsby of Penne's Place, who disposed of it in 1572. After that its history is unclear, but it is unlikely that there was a building on the estate before the nucleus of the present house was constructed in the mid-eighteenth century.

The Aldenham Lodge estate was historically associated with Porters and the Manor of Weld in Shenley Parish, originally going under the name of Sherlands. In 1748 the Manor of Weld was bought by John Mason and the two estates were separated in 1772 when Porters was sold to Lord

76

Howe. The Mason family continued to occupy Aldenham Lodge, although in 1837 the farm of 240 acres was leased to a Medburn farmer named Dickinson. Following the death in 1853 of a later John Mason, who was a Chairman of Quarter Sessions and one of the examining magistrates in the Radlett murder of 1823, the house was leased to Thomas Bagnall, who in 1870 bought the Newberries estate. Aldenham Lodge was then acquired by Thomas Part, succeeded on his death in 1885 by his son, Charles T. Part, who became a great benefactor to the village before he sold up the residue and moved away in 1902.

Some way to the south of Radlett on Watling Street the hamlet of Cobden Hill led a separate existence. The first documented reference to 'a place called Coppedthorne' comes in a quit claim of 1294; later documents show the name evolving through Copthorne Hill to the first use of the present name in a parish register entry of 1629. The chantry chapel erected on the hill in 1510 by Sir Humphrey Coningsby and dissolved in 1552 was followed by a building called Chapel House, which may have been a conversion of the original chapel; it was still standing in 1704. The present Chantry Cottage was built around the beginning of the nineteenth century on the same site; although never itself a chapel it was obviously designed to reflect its predecessor.

A farm appeared on the hilltop in the early nineteenth century. The open square barns were on the north side of a track which now leads to King George V Playing Field, with a small farmhouse — still standing but much enlarged — on the south side. The farm disappeared when the Phillimores, as lords of the manor of Titberst & Kendals, emparked most of the land; a laundry with drying ground was then started up in the back of the house.

About the year 1816 Richard Hooper built a pair of semi-detached cottages on the waste land beside Watling Street, to which a beerhouse licence was attached in 1845; it was then given the name of Cat & Fiddle. Hooper was a brickmaker and also had a lime kiln in a deep dell opposite the farm. Just below the pub, William Kingston had established a bakery some time before 1841, by which year the population of Cobden Hill was 58. In 1865 the hamlet was absorbed into the new Parish of Radlett.

A mile or so further south on Watling Street stood the ancient hamlet of Medburn, of which few traces remain. Medburn Bridge was built in 1769 to carry the Street over the Tykeswater stream, at

The Cat and Fiddle, drawn by Ted Barker.

the joint expense of Robert Phillimore and Thomas Neate, the then lords of the two local manors; it had to be rebuilt around 1830 to allow for the easier passage of stage coaches. Just to the north of the bridge is the Waggon & Horses public house, an old seventeenth century building, licensed as a beerhouse around 1845.

To the east of Medburn, and separated by the Tykeswater, there was another ancient hamlet known as Theobald Street, the name now used only for the road running through the area. Two plausible explanations for the name have been advanced: first, that it is a corruption of the manorial name of Titberst; second, that it derives from Abbot Theobald of Westminster, to whom the lands were demised at about the time of the Norman Conquest. This was an area of mainly small farms: Tilehouse, Cressalls, Organ Hall, Brooklands and Tykeswater, with the old house of Organ Hall not far away. An ancient homestead known as Haydons stood in the fields a few hundred yards east of Organ Hall Farm; the name is probably derived from the Saxon word *heidene*, one of the boundary spots mentioned in the 'Offa' Charter. Some of this area was transferred to the newly-formed Parish of Boreham Wood in 1909.

On the hilltop to the west of Radlett another community established itself at Batlers Green, clustered around the Elizabethan house and separate farmhouse facing it which both bear this name. A survey in 1585 records the house as a homestead with five new barns and stables, two orchards, a garden and other lands totalling 63 acres in all, which was then called Allen Ballardes, presumably after the name of the occupant. There are later references to Ballardes Green before the present form was adopted in the seventeenth century.

The listed Batlers Green House was built around 1560 of plastered timber and brick but was much enlarged and altered in the eighteenth and nineteenth centuries, when a new Georgian brick front was added. Throughout most of its life the house has been occupied by working farmers, although in the 1840s the land was added to the Phillimore estates. By then the farmland amounted to about 275 acres, including most of the area bounded by New Road, Watford Road and Watling Street, on which much of Radlett has subsequently developed. For a number of years early this century the house was lived in by Bobby Phillimore, during which time he established the nearby fruit farm. In the inter-war period it became a private school, then served as a maternity hospital during the last war. More recently it has reverted to private occupation.

Like the house, the original Batlers Green Farm building — now the farm shop — is a listed building, parts of which date back to the seventeenth century. There are no firm records of the farm before 1803, when it extended to some 203 acres and incorporated older farms called Pondsyard, Edmonds and Neales. By that time the lands bounded by New Road and Common Lane had been sold to George Woodford Thellusson of Wall Hall, and they have since remained in the possession of Thellusson's successors, currently the Hertfordshire County Council, and have been worked by various tenant farmers.

New Road was constructed in 1803 to replace several ancient highways across the Great Common Field, which had been stopped up as part of the enclosures of that year. No buildings were constructed along it, however, until the council housing development of the 1920s, which included a general shop and filling station known as Sydneyville Stores (all demolished in 1968 when the present houses were built). The main Batlers Green housing estate and shopping centre is almost entirely a post-Second World War development.

In about 1860 a small National school for girls and infants was built in Loom Lane near its junction with New Road, called Hatch Green after the name of the field on which it was sited, but this was later closed and converted into cottages when the new schools opened in Watling Street; the cottages were demolished in 1970 when Beagle Close was built on the spot.

In 1969 the Batlers Green district was added to the Parish of Radlett.

ABOVE: The centre of Radlett around 1900. BELOW: The old Red Lion
public house in the 1890s; it was demolished in 1904.

ABOVE: A heavy goods vehicle of the day in Watling Street, with the Flint Cottages in the background, 1905. LEFT: The Flint Cottages, in Station Approach. Note the result of raising the level of the former Shenley Road, following the construction of the railway. RIGHT: Charles Part, owner of Aldenham Lodge, local benefactor and founder of the Radlett Industrial Co-operative Society in 1885.

ABOVE: The original Radlett Stores, sited where Barclays Bank now stands.
BELOW: Mr & Mrs Part inaugurating the new drinking fountain in the
Radlett Gardens (given to the village by Mr Part), 1902. (LJB)

ABOVE: Aldenham Lodge, home of the Part family from the 1880s to the
1900s, was converted to a private hotel. It was demolished in the 1960s.
BELOW: The swimming pool at the Hotel in the 1950s.

ABOVE: The centre of Radlett decorated for the wedding of Miss Lucy Part.
BELOW: Bill Andrew's smithy at the rear of the Flint Cottages in the 1890s.

83

'Granny' Palmer stands outside her ancient tumbledown cottage at The Folly, Watford Road, c1905. The building had been condemned but was left until Mrs Palmer's death at the age of 96 in 1918.

ABOVE: Cottagers at Cobden Hill, c1910. BELOW: The Cat & Fiddle
public house and the orphanage buildings at Cobden Hill, c1910.

ABOVE: Children from the orphanage, Cobden Hill. BELOW: At the Furniture Trades Orphanage at Cobden Hill, living accommodation was in the two pairs of semi-detached houses (each now converted into a single private house), with communal facilities in what is now the Masonic Hall, behind the nearer building.

ABOVE: The nucleus of Batlers Green House is a two-bay hall dating from c1500, extended in piecemeal fashion over the centuries in a variety of styles, the most recent addition being the Georgian cross-wing fronting Common Lane. (RCHM) INSET: Original exposed moulded rafters in Batlers Green House. (RCHM) BELOW: Batlers Green Farm: the original 16th century building (which was once much larger than its present size) is on the right, and the modern farmhouse on the left. (RCHM)

ABOVE: The guilty men, from a sketch made during their trial. BELOW:
Probert's Cottage in Gill's Hill Lane, drawn in 1823.

The Radlett Murder

One event briefly and sordidly brought Radlett to the centre stage of public interest in the early nineteenth century. This was the murder of William Weare in Gills Hill Lane on the evening of Friday, 24 October 1823. No single crime had ever excited more attention up to then, and few since. Historian G.M. Trevelyan has described the subsequent trial of the murderers as the event that created the greatest popular interest in Britain between the adultery trial of Queen Caroline and the Reform Bill of 1832. Not only did the circumstances and the characters involved grip the imagination of the whole nation, but the crime itself has possibly generated more persistent interest among writers over the century and a half that has succeeded it than any other.

In outline, the details of the crime are quite simple. John Thurtell, the son of a well-to-do businessman and Mayor of Norwich, who had degenerated into a compulsive gambler and promoter of illegal prizefights, sought revenge on a similar ne'er-do-well called William Weare, who he claimed had cheated him of £300 at a game of cards in a London club. With an accomplice named Joseph Hunt, Thurtell enticed Weare to join them for a shooting weekend in Radlett, staying in a cottage rented by another sleazy character called William Probert. Approaching the cottage, which was sited approximately where Oaks Close now joins Gills Hill Lane, in one of the two gigs hired for the journey, Thurtell, according to a contemporary account 'drew from his bosom the fatal pistol, discharged it in the face of the unsuspecting victim, dashed him out of the gig, pounced upon him like a wild beast, dashed the discharged fire-arm literally through his brains, struggled and struggled, was almost overmastered, drew forth the knife, felt for the vein and divided it'.

The body of the murdered man was dumped, first in a pond in the grounds of Probert's cottage, and then in another pond adjacent to Watling Street, close to the boundary between Elstree and Aldenham Parishes. The murder might have remained undetected but for the alertness of two farm labourers going to work the following morning, who saw Thurtell and Hunt 'grabbing in the hedge' near the scene of the crime, and later themselves returned to the spot where, after a careful search, they discovered the murder weapons. On reporting their find to their employer, Charles Nicholls of Batlers Green Farm, the processes of the law were set in hand and in due course the murderers were arraigned at Hertford Assizes for trial by Grand Jury (the chairman being William Lamb, later Lord Melbourne and a future prime minister).

The subsequent proceedings — one of the first cases in which fair trial and free press collided — were sensational. Throughout the country, an avid readership was held in thrall by gruesome details reported in the burgeoning mass market newspapers. Moralists drew inspiration from the revelations about London's underworld, its prizefighting dens and gambling hells. Details of the crime were played out as popular entertainment in many of the leading theatres of the day, one of which utilised the actual horse and gig which carried Thurtell and Weare, and many broadsheet ballads were composed about it.

Hunt had turned King's Evidence, which did not prevent him from being transported for life to Australia. Thurtell, brazenly denying involvement to the last, was found guilty and publicly hanged before an enormous crowd outside Hertford gaol. The murder cottage in Gills Hill Lane became a national tourist attraction, visited among others by Sir Walter Scott, who described his visit in his published journals. Charles Dickens, George Borrow, Bulwer Lytton, Thomas Carlyle and George Eliot all introduced references to the crime in their writing.

Many histories of the event have subsequently been written, the latest being a comprehensive account by an American, Albert Borowitz — *The Thurtell-Hunt Murder Case.*

The gig in the narrow, overgrown lane — a powerful symbol of the murder, drawn in 1824.

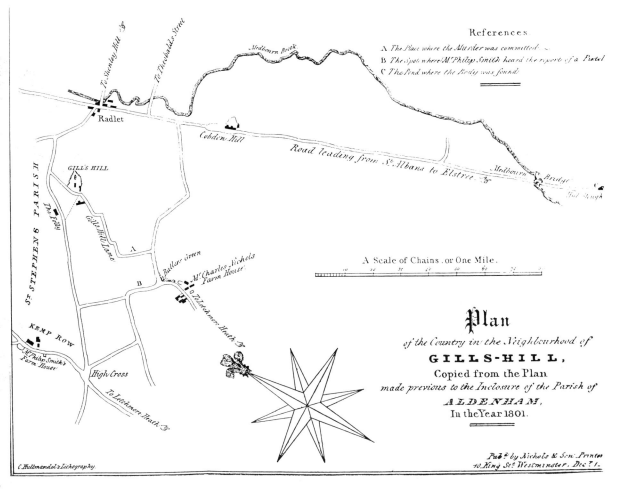

ABOVE: A plan of the murder location, copied from the 1803 enclosure map.
BELOW: An 1824 'depiction' of the recovery of Weares' body from Hill
Slough.

RADLETT, HERTS.
THE KENDALLS ESTATE.

CONVEYANCES FREE OF LAW COSTS. PAYMENTS SPREAD OVER 10 YEARS.

Particulars, Plan & Conditions of Sale
OF
FIFTY-EIGHT PLOTS
OF
FREEHOLD BUILDING LAND
FRONTING

Watling Street, the Main Road to Watford, Aldenham Avenue, and The Crosspath,

SUITABLE FOR THE ERECTION OF WELL-DESIGNED HOUSES
With Good Depths.

Adjoining Radlett Station on the Midland Railway and within easy distance of St. Albans.

EXCELLENT ROADS.   SEWERS LAID.   GOOD WATER SUPPLY.
TITHE FREE & FREE FROM LAND TAX.

Which will be Offered by Auction, by

MR. F. G. WHEATLEY,
IN CONJUNCTION WITH
MR. W. F. INGRAM,

IN A MARQUEE ON THE ESTATE,
On Thursday, the 7th of July, 1898,
At 1.30 o'clock in the Afternoon.

A Limited Number of Return Railway Tickets from Moorgate Station will be issued, on application to the Auctioneer. Price, 2s. 6d. Each.   LUNCHEON PROVIDED AT PLACE OF SALE.

Particulars, Plan and Conditions of Sale can be obtained of Messrs. BURGOYNES, MILNES & GREATBACH, Solicitors, 356, Oxford Street, W.; of Mr. W. F. INGRAM, 2, St. Andrew's Place, Lewes, Sussex; of R. C. PHILLIMORE, Esq., Cobden Hill, Radlett, Herts; and of the Auctioneer, 263, Strand, London, W.C.

Particulars of sale of building plots on the Kendals Estate. It was this sale which marked the beginning of Radlett as a modern residential settlement.

Modern Radlett

In 1864, Christ Church was built (originally to serve as a District Chapelry) on land donated by Captain W.B. Phillimore of Kendal Hall who, together with Thomas Bagnall of Aldenham Lodge and Henry Hucks Gibbs of Aldenham House and others, subscribed towards its cost. On 8 December 1865 the Ecclesiastical Parish of Radlett was created by Order in Council.

Also in 1864, construction started on the extension of the Midland Railway southward from Bedford towards London, and in 1868 the line opened with a station at Radlett. The station was originally going to be called Aldenham, but local pressures ensured that the new Parish was put on the railway map.

These two events fix with some precision the start of the evolution of Radlett as a modern community, but it was not until more than 30 years later, at the turn of the century, that development took off in earnest. In 1871 there were 443 people living in 88 houses in the new Parish, and there were still less than 1,000 people in 1901. Today the population is around 8,000, who live in about 3,500 homes, and the rate of growth is only limited by the strict controls imposed by the Green Belt around Radlett and restrictions on infilling.

The original Church Parish included not only the small settlement around the crossroads which gave it its name, but also the then quite separate district of Cobden Hill, as well as Medburn and the ancient hamlet of Theobald Street, extending nearly to the centre of Boreham Wood. In 1909 this south-eastern section was transferred to the newly-formed Parish of Borehamwood (spelled as one word). The boundaries of Radlett were subsequently enlarged when in 1935 the area of the Newlands estate north of Malt Lane was transferred from St Stephen's Parish, and in 1969 the district around Batler's Green was transferred from Aldenham to fix the limits of present-day Radlett: that is, the built-up area designated as a 'specified settlement' within the Green Belt, though the Church Parish boundaries extend somewhat beyond this especially to the south.

In 1894, when the two Church Parishes were reunited for local government purposes by the formation of a new civil Parish, the Council adopted the historic name of Aldenham as still being the dominant presence within the new territory; change since then has left many newer inhabitants of Radlett confused as to why their Parish Council should bear the name of this small village. The first Annual Parish Council was held in the Parish room at Aldenham vicarage, with meetings of Councillors held in rotation at Aldenham, Letchmore Heath and Radlett. Later, some offices were taken in a building on Watling Street, where the LAP garage now stands, and which also housed the first library, until the present premises were acquired in Aldenham Avenue.

Coincidentally the first elementary school for the boys of Radlett was also built in 1864 at Medburn (together with its twin at Delrow for those in Aldenham) by the Brewers' Company as part of their reorganisation of Aldenham School. For many years Medburn School had a large catchment area, comprising Elstree and Boreham Wood as well as Radlett, and for most pupils there was no alternative to the long trudge along Watling Street. About 100 boys of all ages were taught in a single classroom, later subdivided by a wooden partition, by a headmaster and his two or three assistants. A house for the headmaster formed an integral part of the school. The first head was a Mr Dutton, who was 'translated' from Aldenham Lower School, but the character of the school (and no doubt the boys in it) was formed by the remarkable man who succeeded as headmaster in 1883, and stayed until his retirement 39 years later.

This was Frederick J. Forfeitt, universally known to his charges for rather obscure reasons as 'Dicky'. Although only 26 when he arrived at Medburn, he had previously been headmaster of Chesham boy's school. Harold Knee, a pupil at Medburn from 1905 until 1909, recalls: 'Dicky was a wonderful headmaster and adept at instilling the three Rs into our thick skulls. What he didn't achieve by exhortation he did by sundry knocks on the back of our heads; he had a large gold ring on his finger which almost dented our craniums when we were the recipients of his "favours". We were a pretty boisterous lot but Dicky was a good disciplinarian and kept our youthful spirits in check'.

From the outset, Forfeitt played an active role in the development of the village as well as the school. One of the originators of the Radlett Cricket Club in 1884, he was the secretary and a playing member for many years. For 22 years he was choirmaster at Christ Church, and read the lessons regularly. In 1893 he became secretary of the Radlett Stores, which was founded as a cooperative society, and the following year he became a founder-member of the Parish Council. Later on, acquiring an interest in friendly society work, he started the local branch of the National Deposit Friendly Society and became its secretary.

Dicky must have been an almost God-like figure to the pupils in his care, and thanks to his enthusiasm Medburn achieved scholastic successes beyond the normal run of a village school, which perforce accommodated mainly those boys whose parents could not afford a private schooling. Harold Knee again: 'We were a pretty ragged-looking lot. The majority of boys wore patched clothing, had only one pair of boots to their name, and almost invariably had nits in their hair . . . fleas abounded and could be picked up almost anywhere . . . sanitation was still pretty crude and earth closets there were in plenty. But although there were rags, hardship and distress and quite a number of families were below the poverty line, the majority of children were fed on good, plain, honest grub'. Some of the enthusiasm of Dicky Forfeitt for his school shines through in his end-of-term reports, which invariably included a commentary on current events and noteworthy achievements, including the problems of keeping the school going during the First World War.

After Forfeitt's retirement in 1922, Medburn School continued to provide elementary education in its cramped Victorian premises right up to the 1950s. The school building remains much in its original state and is now used as boarding kennels, the main classroom having been retained until recently, quite unrestored.

A girls' school was built at the foot of Loom Lane in 1878, also financed by the Platt Charity of the Brewers' Company, and this also survived under similar cramped conditions until the 1950s. The equivalent of Mr Forfeitt was Governess Mary Burchett, usually referred to as 'Gov': an equally impressive and long-serving headmistress, and also a leading figure in Parish affairs. At one time the girls at the school were required to wear red-riding-hood cloaks, donated by the Platt Charity. Since its closure, the school buildings have served as a youth centre. The first infants' school for five- to seven-year-olds was opened nearby in Cobden Hill in 1902, with Miss F.A. Quartermaine as headmistress, and remained in service until quite recently. All the local schools were administered by the Church of England until the Education Act of 1944.

Under the post-war schools modernisation programme, new primary schools have been built at Fairfield and Newberries, and a new infants' school at Gills Hill Lane, but Radlett children still have to travel out of the Parish from the age of eleven, to continue in secondary and further education within the State sector.

The railway came to Radlett in 1868, not because a new company saw prospects for exploiting this part of the London hinterland, but because a relatively long-established company, the Midland Railway, based at Derby and operating throughout the East Midlands, wished to achieve its own link with London. Previously the Midland Railway had its own rails only as far south as Bedford and, for connections to London, was dependent on running facilities over the lines of other companies *via* Rugby to Euston or *via* Hitchin to Kings Cross. Increasing chaos as traffic grew, and disputes over priorities, led the Midland Railway to obtain an Act of Parliament in 1863 for its own line, running from Bedford *via* Luton and St Albans into a new London terminus at St Pancras. The route south of St Albans was selected naturally by the valley of the Tykeswater, and the decision to site a station at the then tiny hamlet of Radlett had profound, though delayed, consequences for the future growth of the settlement.

The line was opened on 13 July 1868, initially as far as Kentish Town, with running facilities from there over Metropolitan Railway lines into Moorgate and then, a few months later, from 1 October 1868, into the impressive new terminus at St Pancras. The stations were built from the outset with four tracks but the rest of the line with only two tracks. Provision was made for widening to the present four-track system, which took place in the 1880s.

Thus Radlett acquired its station on the Midland main line almost by accident, and in the earliest days it was viewed more as a convenient distribution point for goods and passengers in the rural areas than as serving any purely local needs. Although it enjoyed a good service of stopping trains right from the start, it is unlikely it saw any major traffic movements before 1900. Nevertheless, the station was constructed with all the accessories of its Victorian kind, complete with coal sidings, a goods depôt, water tower with pumping machinery, and a separate luggage bay (sited where the Oakway car hire depôt now stands), whose greatest single use was the transit of passengers' unaccompanied luggage to and from house parties at local mansions and the boarding school at Aldenham. One early use was to convey gravel, clay and chalk from local mineral workings, and the first edition of the Ordnance Survey map of 1871 shows a network of tramway lines, running down the hillside from the gravel pits on Shenley Hill and into the goods sidings. The gradients were of course too steep for locomotives, and so horse or human muscle power formed the main means of propelling the empty trucks up the hill, to descend when full under gravity.

The first passenger trains to Radlett were mainly third-class four-wheel carriages, not much better than cattle trucks, with wooden bench seats. Many of the box-like vehicles were roofless, and an advertisement of the time laid special emphasis on the fact that excursion trains would have covered roofs. In 1875, the old wooden 'thirds' were scrapped and were replaced by upholstered former 'seconds', a class which was then abolished throughout the Midland system. At the same time, fares were reduced to a more affordable level. The standard carriage soon became a six-wheeler composite of first and third classes, with four or five compartments in each and partitions right up to the roof. Further improvements followed progressively until, by the turn of the century, daily commuting to London became almost as tolerable as at the present day, save for the dirt and pollution inevitably linked with steam locomotion. The locomotives which hauled the trains were a mixture of 2-4-0 tender engines for St Pancras trains and 4-4-0 condensing tank engines for the Moorgate service, with its final underground stretch. Designed by the Midland's celebrated chief mechanical engineer, Matthew Kirtley, in the 1860s, they remained (with modifications introduced by Kirtley's successor, S.W. Johnson) the principal motive power on the line until well into the present century.

Passenger steam trains on the Bedford line came to an end in the early 1960s with the introduction of the diesel multiple units of recent and generally unloved memory, with their propensity to catch fire at the slightest malfunction while in service, and in the early 1980s the whole line to Bedford was electrified. Goods traffic had long since disappeared from the Radlett scene, and in 1989 the last vestiges of the old station layout vanished with the demolition of the goods shed, the little weighhouse and the remaining, derelict coal bay. The station buildings themselves had been completely reconstructed in the early 1980s as part of the electrification plans.

In 1871 there was only a thin sprinkling of buildings in Radlett: the mansions of Newberries, Aldenham Lodge and Kendals Hall, and their lodges and bothies, the Church and its vicarage, the station complex, and the three public houses, and a few small groups of terraced houses. These were the Primrose Cottages at the foot of the Watford Road, the Flint Cottages at the Station Approach and The Terrace along Watling Street, as well as a number of straggling cottages on Cobden Hill and the two old thatched dwellings called Lambeth Cottages at the foot of Shenley Hill. There was also a number of farm houses at Darnhills, Cobden Hill and Kendals Pound. In the outlying areas, there were isolated dwellings at The Folly on Watford Road and in Gills Hill Lane (where Probert's murder cottage also still stood, though probably unoccupied).

By the time the area was resurveyed in 1896, little had changed. Watling Street itself was still hardly more than a cart track. The girls' school and an adjacent house (Church Cottage) had been built at the foot of Loom Lane; a few houses had been erected at the foot of Shenley Hill, and those on The Terrace rebuilt; a shop, post office and social club provided by Charles Part of Aldenham Lodge in 1884 existed near the station in Watling Street, along with a small dairy run by Part's bailiff, Mr Bayliss, and the lines of Station Road and Park Road had just been laid out, with a few houses already built, following the sale of farmland near the Red Lion for speculative building. This land sale also opened up development along Watling Street, north of the Red Lion. In the main Radlett still slumbered, unaware that its days as a backwater were numbered.

On Thursday 7 July 1898 Radlett awoke. Bobby Phillimore of Kendals Hall, who then owned nearly half Radlett's acreage, offered at auction (held in a marquee on the estate) about two hundred acres of land to the west of Watling Street, divided into separate plots. The sale details provided for new roads called Aldenham Avenue and The Crosspath. The 58 plots went for prices from £125 for a prime site on Watling Street and £115 in Aldenham Avenue, through £30–£50 in The Crosspath, to £25–£30 for plots on Watford Road. Subsequently the Kendals Estate Office was set up, with premises in Scrubbitts Square, to continue the sale of land for development.

As part of these comprehensive development plans, Mr Phillimore laid out an area to be called Scrubbitts Square (after the name of the old wood in the locality) on which were built blocks of flats to be let at low rents to local agricultural and railway workers: an early example of a philanthropic housing scheme for the working classes, for which he had been enthused by his fellow LCC Councillor and Fabian, Sidney Webb, and Radlett resident Fred Knee, who founded the Workmen's National Housing Council in 1898. For many years these flats served a useful social purpose in an area of otherwise middle-class housing but, with the passage of time, they became decrepit and, being incapable of modernisation, were demolished in the 1970s to be replaced by the present modern flats run by a housing association.

Not to be outdone, Phillimore's fellow land-owner, Charles Part, soon afterwards followed suit and put substantial areas of his Aldenham Lodge estate to the east of Watling Street and north of Shenley Hill on the market for similar housing development. His own philanthropy had taken the form of giving land to the village for a parish hall and another plot to serve as a recreation ground: the present Radlett Gardens. A centrepiece of the recreation ground was an elaborate canopied drinking fountain, also financed by Mr Part, first installed in commemoration of Queen Victoria's golden jubilee and further embellished in 1902.

With all this land suddenly available for high-class housing development, builders had a bonanza, especially when parts of the Newlands estate (then in the adjacent parish of St Stephens) were also added. Many of the bigger houses were built by the Wiggs Brothers, whose father, George Wiggs, had set up as a builder in Watford in about 1883 and who started building in Radlett around 1900. George's son, William, opened an office in Watling Street in 1911 and, after the First World War, he was joined by brother Walter. The brothers built The Grove estate; many of the houses in Newlands, Goodyers and Oakridge Avenues; some of the large ones in The Avenue and The

Warren, and a number in Loom Lane, Christchurch Crescent and Watford Road. William Wiggs retired in 1952 but Walter carried on until the sixties, when he sold the office, the family house Osta, and builder's yard to LAP Motors for the erection of the present garage. In the late 1920s the brothers took over the Parish Hall, and converted it into a comfortable cinema, well patronised until it eventually went the way of most in the face of television in the 1960s; the premises then reverted to their original function.

Other local builders contributed to the development: Harry Wootton, who started up in 1895 and for many years had his office and works in Station Road, and Fred Slade and his son, who mainly lent the finishing touches rather than handling the basic construction work, and whose premises at Slade's Yard behind The Terrace have only recently been taken over for redevelopment as 25 retirement flats. When E.N. Grace set up his estate agent's office in one of the Flint Cottages before the First World War, he became the sole agent for most of the major estate developments, and also organised the building of some large new houses; he was succeeded as agent by H. Coward, operating from nearby premises (now Cormack's).

The third major land-owner in Radlett, George Miller of Newberries, who owned the land to the south of Shenley Hill and east of Theobald Street, did not part with any of his property before he vacated the estate in the 1930s. The purchaser, Sir Arthur du Cros, immediately started to break up the estate for development but, before much could happen, the Second World War intervened. After the war, the land was acquired by William Old & Company, who proceeded to lay out a large housing estate with the new roads of William's Way and Craigweil Avenue following the line of the original carriage drives, and the lengthy Newberries Avenue running transversely across the parkland; this was completed by the 1960s. At about that time, the last area of former farmland within Radlett — the remains of the historic Darnhills (or Darnells) Farm — were given over to the development of two large blocks of flats, and Darnhills House itself was demolished.

Further housing development since the last war has consisted mainly of infilling within the boundaries of the Green Belt, which were defined in the 1940s by the limits of the then existing housing stock. Much of the recent building has been in the nature of small estates and individual houses by speculative builders and property companies, but the north-west corner of Radlett at Batlers Green has seen the completion of a relatively large development by the local authority, which had been started in the inter-war period. Most of the early council stock along New Road has been demolished and replaced and, sadly, many more recent flats put up by industrialised building techniques in the 1960s proved to be of such appallingly poor quality that they have had to be demolished, and replaced within a twenty-year life span.

By the start of the Second World War in 1939, the number of dwellings in Radlett had risen to about 800 mainly large detached houses in substantial, leafy grounds. Fifty years later this number has grown to over 3,000, and to many of the older inhabitants, who recall the days when the average housing plot ran to an acre or more, the village now seems to be bursting at the seams. However, new plots seem continually to be conjured out of thin air (or more strictly, thick back gardens) to meet the insatiable demand for high-quality houses in this most desirable of environments, and recent planning controls seeking to limit the rate of growth to one hundred new houses per five-year period have had only limited success in holding back the creeping urbanisation of Radlett. At a time when five houses to the acre is seen as the norm in even the most verdant corners of this once rural community, the scope for backland and cul-de-sac development seems potentially such as to destroy, stealthily but steadily, the very character of the settlement which has made it such a sought-after place, unless tighter and more stringent controls on development are enforced. At the same time, the economic forces which have pushed house prices up, until they are among the most expensive in the land outside London, have meant that acquiring a house of their own in their native community is now out of the question for most of the sons and daughters of long-established Radlett residents who, in consequence, are obliged to move out of the district in order to find affordable houses.

Places for religious worship also proliferated after 1900. The Parish Church of Christ Church itself, though more than adequate for parishioners when built in 1864, became uncomfortably inadequate for the rapidly expanding population. In 1905 a decision was taken to double its capacity, adding a new nave and chancel, new vestries and an organ chamber: the consecration of the new part took place on 14 November 1907 by the Bishop of St Albans. The church hall was built in 1928 and extended in the 1970s. The Glebe Field, a meadow of one-and-a-half acres behind the Church, was purchased by a group of church members in 1959 and presented to the Church as a joint bequest, thereby securing an open lung for the village, safe from development.

In 1903, a galvanised iron and wooden structure which had previously seen service in St Albans was put up in Station Road as a Methodist Chapel and social centre. It served its purpose for thirty-five years, until the present church building was constructed on the site in 1938. With the merging of the various non-conformist Christian sects this has now become the United Free Church.

A Congregational Church was opened in a hall on Watling Street in 1905 and a replacement building on the same site was consecrated in 1930. Later, after merger with the Presbyterian Church, it became known as the United Reform Church and later still it merged with the Wesleyan Church, at which time the Watling Street building became redundant. The building is now used as a Reform Synagogue for members of the Jewish faith.

The Roman Catholic Church was established in The Crosspath in 1910 by public subscription, a somewhat surprising subscriber being George Bernard Shaw (then living in St Albans) who, when approached by the priest-in-charge, donated the not inconsiderable sum for those days of £10. In 1953, a final bequest of land by the Phillimore family provided the site for a second Church of England building at Gills Hill Lane, which formed a combined place of worship and social hall, further extended in 1988. A church of the Plymouth Brethren was built in Willow Way in 1955.

Today, the main churches of Radlett operate in unison through the Radlett Ecumenical Church Council: a far cry from the ill-concealed hostility between sects earlier this century.

Alongside the rapid post-1900 development of housing in Radlett there was a parallel growth in shopping and commercial services. Radlett's second shop, a bakery run by Henry Cole, who moved into it from his earlier premises in High Cross, had opened in 1896 near the Red Lion. Next door, William Andrews had transferred his smithy from its earlier premises at the rear of the Flint Cottages. The two early tradesmen are commemorated in a tablet bearing the initials WA - HC and the date 1896 set high in the wall above the baker's shop, which still remains today under different ownership, though the smithy closed down in 1913 when Mr Andrews' grandsons, Charles and Harry Howard, converted the premises into a garage for the new motor trade.

The shop started by Charles Part in 1884 had early on become the Radlett Industrial Societies Limited, a co-operative store registered under the Friendly Societies Acts, with Mr Part as the President of the management committee. He had come from a Lancashire family and knew something of the benefits of the co-operative concerns flourishing in the north. He was a persistent advocate of co-operative principles and often urged their adoption upon farmers and agriculturists. The Society moved into new premises across the road and next to the bakery in 1902, and the shop became known as the Radlett Stores. At first it retained its post office work but, as this expanded and more room was required for telegraphic business, it was transferred into the first full post office, housed in the rival Porter's ironmongers and general stores at the corner of Station Road.

The Radlett Stores was an emporium for local people run by their representatives. Among the notable villagers associated with it were Frederick ('Dicky') Forfeitt, secretary of the Society for about 40 years from 1892, John Burrell, chairman of the management committee for more than 20 years, and Frederick Watson (a signalman on the railway line at Cobden Hill for most of his working life) who, after a long period on the committee, succeeded Mr Part as President when the latter died in 1928. In 1930, the Stores extended onto an adjacent vacant plot, which it had prudently acquired at the outset, and later it was merged into the expanding London Co-operative Society. After serving the local population well for nearly a hundred years it finally closed, in the face of fierce competition from new supermarkets in the surrounding towns, in 1980. Today, however, the premises are once again operating as a general store.

In 1903, the association of the Wing family with the old Red Lion public house came to an end, when 'young' Tom died, and his widow was persuaded to sell it to the newly-formed and locally based Hertfordshire Public House Trust, which had Alex Part (the son of Charles) as its managing director. The old inn was demolished and the present Red Lion hotel was built on the site in 1905 by the Trust. After amalgamation with other county trusts, the owners changed their name to the Home Counties Trust and in 1915 a new head office for the organisation was built next to the Red Lion. Two years later the offices were moved to central London and, with further amalgamations following shortly afterwards, the name of Trust Houses Limited was adopted, the forerunner of today's mighty Trust House Forte concern, which truly can be said to have had its genesis in Radlett. The former offices are now the restaurant and bedroom block of the hotel.

The shopping centre spread out in several directions from its nucleus around the Red Lion. Just above the inn in Aldenham Road a short row of shops was built in 1904, among them the grocery business of Henry Fish, formerly the manager of the Radlett Stores. Such was his success that within a year or so he was able to transfer to another more imposing shop in Watling Street, where he quickly built up a quality business, catering for the occupants of the new large houses in the vicinity. Within a few years more he sold out to International Stores Limited, which continued to trade there until the 1960s.

Between Henry Fish's stores and the long-established Railway Inn (formerly known as the Cross Keys) a parade of shops quickly followed. The existing cottages on The Terrace, some of them already housing tradesmen, were converted into shops in 1906, their front gardens replaced by a tarmac surface right down to the road. The original tradesmen in The Terrace, some of whom continued in business until fairly recent times, were Albert Heaver (newsagent and confectioner), William Wilson (saddler), William Rufus Allen (bootmaker), Rodney Stephens (butcher), William Picton (tea rooms), and Fred Lamb (fishmonger). In 1912, a greengrocers' shop was built for George Hill and Sons, who had started as nurserymen and landscape gardeners on the Watford Road some years previously, following the sale of the Aldenham Lodge estate, on which George Hill had been employed as a gardener: this was run by the family until 1959, when it was sold to S.P. Draper.

The Old Vicarage, Radlett, drawn by Ted Barker.

Opposite the Red Lion a small group of shops was built next to the Flint Cottages. The corner shop was opened for 'haute couture' by Mrs Mark Hall, the wife of the stationmaster, and next door a barber's shop was established by Walter Massey bearing the legend 'Patronised by His Royal Highness Prince Louis of Battenberg'. The Prince, father of the late Earl Mountbatten, had stayed at Kendals Hall for some months in 1904 and Walter had attended to his tonsorial requirements. Next to Massey's was a sweet shop run by the Gamble sisters, and a few years later a chemist's was opened by a Mr Freeman.

Other shops spread out north of the Red Lion on Watling Street, including Crawley's (later Holdham's) butcher's shop on one corner of Station Road, with its distinctive canopy supported on iron pillars stretching out on to the pavement; Porter's shop was on the other corner but faded out in the mid-thirties, when its postal business was transferred to the new purpose-built post office at the south end of the shopping centre. By the start of the First World War nearly fifty shops had been established.

In about 1894, builders' merchants Pratt's of Watford opened a depôt in Radlett next to the station. The yard manager was John Burrell, whose father had held a similar position in Watford. A few years later the business was bought by Bobby Phillimore of Kendals Hall who, with Burrell as his managing partner, set up Kendals Brick & Lime firm, with offices in Station Approach and a brickfield with kilns close to Moses Dell at Cobden Hill, thereby re-establishing a local industry after a gap of more than fifteen hundred years. To transport the bricks down to the main road at Watling Street a light railway was built: this was a great attraction to the boys at Medburn School and a source of many complaints to the headmaster. The firm prospered but, with Bobby's death in 1919, John Burrell chose to retire. He then applied himself to improving the fortunes of the coal and building materials business started up by his eldest son, Tom, and his daughter, Madge, in an office in Wiggs' yard in Watling Street in 1922; it is still a thriving family concern.

John Burrell was one of Radlett's leaders during its rapid expansion after 1900. He was a founder-member of the fire brigade in 1905 and later became the captain. As people's churchwarden at Christ Church he closely supervised the major extension of 1907; a function he repeated nearly thirty years later when the Wesleyan Church was built. He was district councillor on the Board of Guardians and treasurer of the Men's Temperance Society. One of his more notable community services was to rescue the Radlett Stores from financial collapse in the 1900s, by taking over the chairmanship and personally guaranteeing the continued payment of dividends. A completely self-taught and self-made man, he died in 1943 at the age of 79.

In 1898 a branch of Marten, Part & Company, private bankers of St Albans, had been established in Charles Part's original shop, opening on Wednesdays and Fridays only. When the shop moved across the road in 1902 the premises were leased to the bank with an option to purchase the freehold. In 1908 the private bank was absorbed by Barclay's who started a full-time banking service. A completely new bank building was erected on the site in 1934. The Westminster Bank opened a newly-built office on The Terrace in 1913, on the site of the former tea rooms next to the Railway Inn. The National Provincial Bank later had an office on the other side of Watling Street, which was closed on the amalgamation with Westminster Bank.

Further shopping development in the inter-war period was largely confined to the new parade at the north end of Radlett known as The Oakway, built in 1924 and comprising some twenty shops. In the days before car parking was a problem, this new parade flourished, and attracted much of the trade previously carried out nearer the centre. Shortly before the start of the Second World War a block of four shops with flats above, in a distinctive thirties style, was built near the memorial, but the advent of war meant further development of what became Newberries Parade was deferred until the fifties and sixties. By then the prevailing style was faceless modernism, the result being an intrusive and over-large suburban-style shopping parade, now recognised to be quite incompatible with the character of the area as a whole, and which, more than anything else, has urbanised the traditional village centre and posed the question 'Radlett — town or village?'.

Particulars.

THE KENDALLS ESTATE.

·····························

The Estate is pleasantly situated on the main road from St. Albans to London, and adjoins Radlett Station on the Midland Railway, fifteen miles from London and five from St. Albans. Marble Arch is a fourteen miles drive through lovely country.

The Estate has been in the possession of the Phillimore family for generations, and this is the first auction sale of land that has taken place on the Estate.

Radlett is the first station N.W. of London off the clay. The soil is loamy and in places the gravel is on the surface. The subsoil is chalk.

Season Tickets are issued by the Midland Railway for three months at £2 12s. 6d. It is expected that when the Kentish Town extension is completed there will be a greatly improved train service.

The Sewers are laid in the new roads and there will be no cost for sewers to the purchasers of lots in these roads.

The district is well supplied with water by the Colne Valley Company, and their mains are already on the Estate.

There is a great demand for houses in this lovely district, and this is the first opportunity of obtaining land as the property all round belongs to large landowners, who do not care to sell small portions of their estates.

It is intended to throw open to the public at some future time Scrubbitts Wood or part thereof.

There is a good laundry at Radlett.

The Plots are offered for sale as **FREE AS IS POSSIBLE FROM ALL RESTRICTIONS,** excepting such as are mutually advantageous to Vendor and Purchaser.

Possession will be given on payment of £10 per cent. of the purchase money as deposit ; the balance bearing interest at the rate of £4 per cent. may be paid by equal half-yearly payments, if desired, extending over 10 years, but the whole may be paid off at any time on three months' notice.

A CONVEYANCE FREE OF LAW COSTS, OF ANY NUMBER OF LOTS,

WILL BE GIVEN TO EACH PURCHASER.

The Kendals Estate sale.

101

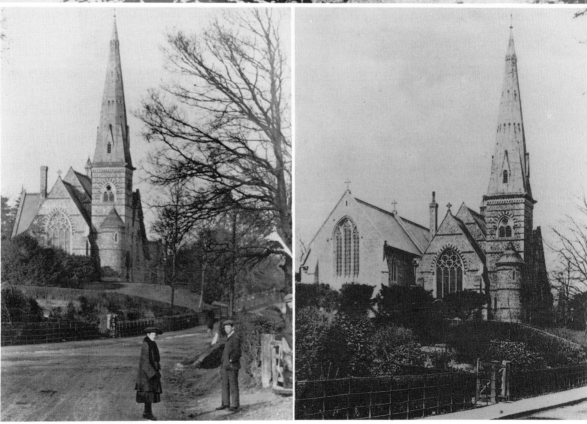

ABOVE: Christ Church and the original vicarage (now demolished) were still in rural surroundings at the turn of the century. LEFT: Christ Church before 1907 had a single nave. RIGHT: After 1907 there was a second, larger nave. A new chancel, vestries and organ chamber were also added.

ABOVE: Radlett Band of Hope meeting in the vicarage garden, 1902. Two of Radlett's leading villagers during its period of rapid growth: LEFT: John Burrell: managing partner of Kendal's Brick & Lime Firm; captain of the Fire Brigade; churchwarden; chairman of the management committee of the Radlett Stores. (JO) RIGHT: F.J. ('Dicky') Forfeitt: headmaster of Medburn School for nearly 40 years; secretary of the Radlett Stores for a similar period; choirmaster at Christ Church; secretary of the Radlett Cricket Club.

ABOVE: The first Congregational Church, built in 1905. BELOW: The replacement Congregational Church, built in front of the earlier one in 1930; now the Jewish Reform Synagogue. OPPOSITE ABOVE: Medburn School group in 1908, and BELOW: in 1920.

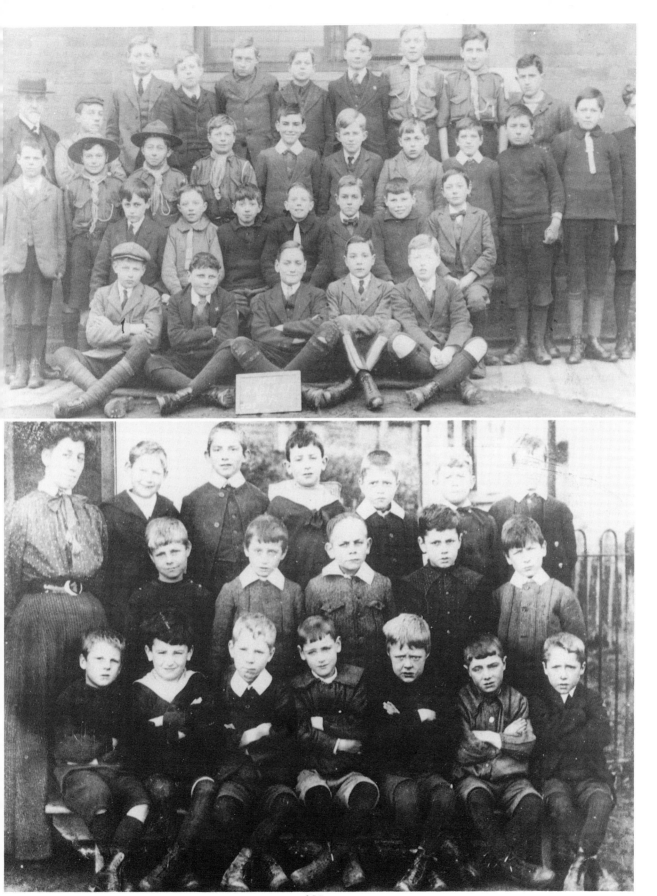

ABOVE: Southern end of The Terrace, Watling Street, soon after the construction of the shopping parade in 1905; the double-fronted building housed Henry Fish's grocery business. BELOW: The International Stores bought Henry Fish's business around 1912 and continued to trade in the premises until the 1960s.

ABOVE: The Railway Inn, seen from the bottom of Shenley Hill c1910.
BELOW: Another view of the Railway Inn (which was formerly called The
Cross Keys). Policemen were more in evidence in those days!

ABOVE: Watling Street soon after the construction of the new Red Lion Hotel. BELOW: Porter's grocery and hardware stores on the corner of Station Road. It housed the post and telegraph office until the present post office was built in the 1930s. OPPOSITE LEFT: The 'new' premises for the Radlett Stores opened in 1902. CENTRE: The extension to the Radlett Stores, completed in 1930, which later became part of the London Co-operative Society. RIGHT: Advertisement for the Radlett Stores in 1927. BELOW: View over Radlett from Scrubbitts Park Road, c1909.

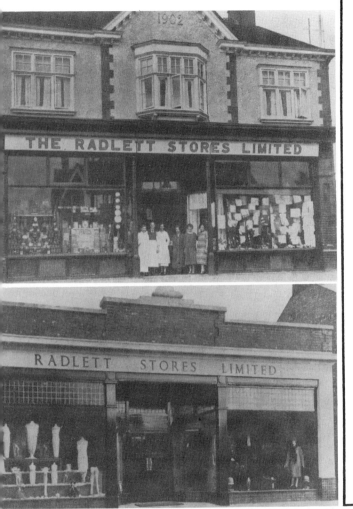

109

ABOVE: Watling Street, at the junction with Station Road, c1915. LEFT:
The Radlett Gardens in the 1920s. RIGHT: Radlett's first library opened in a
hut next to the Gardens in 1934.

ABOVE: The fountain awaiting demolition following the widening of Watling Street in 1942. BELOW: The Crosspath in 1910.

ABOVE: Aldenham Avenue, soon after the first houses were constructed.
BELOW: Looking up Loom Lane, with Church Cottage on the right.

ABOVE: Shenley Hill, c1910. BELOW: Radlett's first fire station.

ABOVE: Radlett Fire Brigade with new motorised truck and early horse-drawn engine in 1927. BELOW: Looking towards Radlett station, with the bridge carrying the drive to Aldenham Lodge in the foreground, c1880. The main line was then only double track; the rails on the left are part of the mineral lines bringing sand and gravel from quarries on Shenley Hill.

ABOVE: Radlett station in 1909. The original buildings were demolished c1980 when the station was rebuilt prior to electrification of the line. BELOW: View over Radlett station.

ABOVE: The stationmaster's house in 1917. (FWS) BELOW: The railway weighhouse and weighbridge, demolished 1989. OPPOSITE ABOVE: A Johnson Class 3 4-4-0 locomotive and tender no 555 at the head of a local train to St Pancras at Radlett station c1930. (FWS) BELOW: The Radlett station staff in 1917. (FWS)

117

ABOVE: Unveiling of the Radlett war memorial. BELOW: Scouts parade in
Watling Street in the 1920s.

ABOVE: Land cleared for construction of The Oakway shopping parade,
1923. (FWS) BELOW: The Oakway shops in the 1950s.

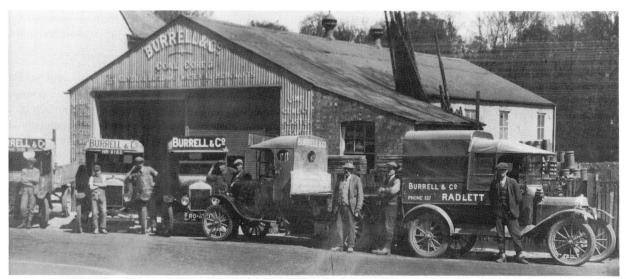

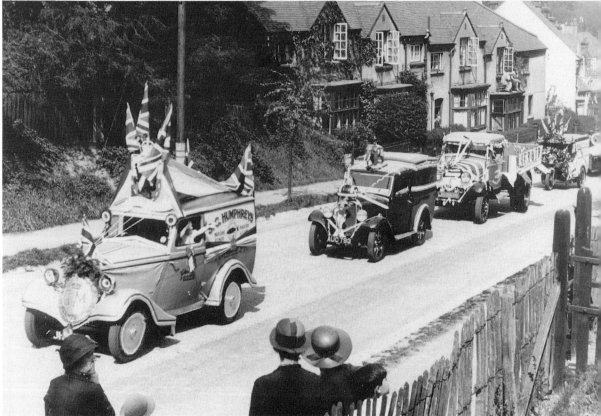

ABOVE: The Burrell fleet in 1922. (JO) BELOW & OPPOSITE ABOVE:
Part of the King George V Jubilee parade in Upper Station Road, 1935.
(FWS) BELOW: Radlett Football ... 1922.

Radlett home guard at Porter's Park in 1942.

ABOVE: The first golf clubhouse at Porter's Park, BELOW: goes up in
flames in 1954.

ABOVE: Netherwylde Farm in 1921. (FWS) BELOW: Newlands House in 1924 (before Newlands Avenue was constructed). (FWS) OPPOSITE ABOVE: Starveacres after the fire, 1929. (FWS) Cricket at Newberries, 1926, in Radlett's green and pleasant land. (FWS)

Men's club outing 1923.

Bibliography

Avery, J.R. *The story of Aldenham House* (Aldenham, 1961)

Borowitz, Albert *The Thurtell-Hunt Murder Case* (Robson Books, 1988)

Brown, W. Newman *Wider reconstitution: family reconstitution in Aldenham* Local Population Studies (No 7, 1971)

Brown, W. Newman *The receipt of poor relief and family situation, Aldenham, Hertfordshire 1630–90* Chapter in 'Land, kinship and life-cycle', ed Smith, R.M. (Cambridge 1984)

Cole, Gilbert *Historic brickfield at Radlett* Hertfordshire Countryside (No 30, 1953) pp 66–67

Coppock, J.T. *Dormitory settlements around London: Radlett* Section in 'Greater London', ed Coppock, J.T. & Prince, H.C. (London 1964)

Cussans, J.E. *History of Hertfordshire, Volume 3* (London 1881)

Dulley, A.J.F. *Housing and society in Aldenham* Hertfordshire Archaeology, Vol VI (St Albans 1977)

Dulley, Franklyn *The old houses of Aldenham* Hertfordshire Countryside (No 211, 1976) pp 28–29

Dulley, Franklyn *Migration in a Georgian parish* Hertfordshire Countryside (No 266, 1981) p 40

Dulley, Franklyn *Nurse-children: a forgotten cottage industry* Hertfordshire Countryside (No 274, 1982) pp 14–15

Foley, H.J. *Rural rambles: the Hertfordshire borders* (London 1889)

Gibbs, K.F. *The parish registers of Aldenham 1559–1659* (Aldenham 1902)

Gibbs, K.F. *The parish registers of Aldenham 1660–1812* (Aldenham 1910)

Hilditch, Neville *A literary jubilee in Hertfordshire* Hertfordshire Countryside (No 126, 1969) pp 36–37

Hussey, C. *Aldenham House* Country Life (23 February 1924) pp 282–290

Knee, Harold J. *Some aspects of the history of Radlett and its surroundings* Typescript (Aldenham 1974)

Knee, Harold J. *The manor of Aldenham — 13th century* Hertfordshire Countryside (No 204, 1976) p 27

Lawrence, Andrew *The Aldenham House gardens* (Aldenham 1989)

Levett, A.E. *Studies in manorial history* (Oxford 1938)

Lorimer, George *Radlett shopkeepers — the early years* Hertfordshire Countryside (No 296, 1984) pp 28–31

Page, W. *A Roman pottery kiln found in Radlett* Procs of the Society of Antiquaries of London (Vol XVII, 1897)

Page, W. (ed) *Victoria County History of Hertfordshire* (London 1908)

Page, W. *A history of the manor of Wall Hall* Typescript (St Albans 1920)

Ritson, G.R.S. *The church of St John the Baptist* (Aldenham 1981)

Saul, J.E. *Radlett past and present* (Radlett 1927)

Spain, Stephen *Shades of Nelson* Hertfordshire Countryside (No 303, 1984) p 18

Tongue, A.H. *The scrag-end of Hertfordshire* Hertfordshire Countryside (No 59, 1961) pp 112–113

Key to Caption Credits

FWS	F.W. Stingemore (negative in HCRO collection)
HCRO	Hertfordshire County Record Office
IS	Ian Sutherland
JO	Joan Oakesmonger
LA	Lord Aldenham
LJB	Mrs L.J. Barton
NMM	National Maritime Museum
PRO	Public Record Office
RCHM	Royal Commission on Historic Monuments
SM	Simon Miller
VM	Verulamium Museum
WA	Westminster Abbey

Subscribers

Presentation Copies

1 Aldenham Parish Council
2 The Radlett Society & Green Belt Association
3 Hertsmere District Council
4 Hertfordshire County Record Office
5 Aldenham School

6 Donald & Margaret Wratten
7 Mark Wratten
8 Isobel Hardwicke
9 Clive & Carolyn Birch
10 Mary & Dennis Broughton
11 Mrs O. Hurt
12 D.L. Johnston
13
15 R. Grindlay
16 Mrs Stella Hunt
17 Mr & Mrs P.C. Marley
18 Miss R. Flawn
19 Mrs J. Wilson
20 Mrs Draper
21 B.S. Thompson
22 Mrs J. Smith
23 W.A. Kellaway
24 Philip & Hilary Booth
25 Mrs T.D. Jeens
26 Mrs Judith Graham
27 Giles Turner
28 Mrs R.G. Freeman
29 John & Pauline Wilson
30 Mr & Mrs Richard Ufland
31 Mr & Mrs L.W. Major
32 Mr & Mrs K.R. Iremonger
33 K. Walter
34 G.J. Child
35 Mrs R.M. Crouch
36
37 Audrey Ashby
38 Penelope J. Brown
39 Victoria & Albert Museum
40 London Guildhall Library
41 Charles K. Brown
42 E.F. Jones
43 Dennis Joss
44 Mr & Mrs G. Bell
45 Pamela Glover
46 Stephen Castle
47 B.C. James
48 Mary Hanson

49 V.R. Khanna
50 Edward Stebbing
51 Philip Eastburn
52
55 Miss M. Kiff
56 Richard Hardy
57 Aldenham Parish Council
58 C.J. Wilkins
59 R.K. Jefferis
60 R.G. Dunscombe
61 A.M. Dunscombe
62 M.R. Mitzman
63
64 Simon E.C. Miller
65 Miss Kathy Tipper
66 Derek & Norman Tipper
67 M.C. Blundell
68 C.F. Spencer
69 P. Jackson
70 Janet Yarrow
71 Mrs B.P. Mackay
72 Radlett Cricket Club
73 Betty M. Hampton
74 A.J.I. Jennings
75 C. Hawkshaw
76 Mr & Mrs Brian Bennett
77 Mr & Mrs Paul Haworth
78 J. David Moore
79 The Hon Diana Holland-Hibbert
80 Charles H. Burton
81 John Rivaz
82 Mrs Gill Shostak
83 Mrs Ros Rivaz
84 Mrs Joan Cousins
85 James Nash Thurgood
86 D.E. Price
87 Mr & Mrs Dennis C. Smith
88 Mrs R.J. Floate
89 Aldenham School
90 Lawrence Woodley
91 Mr & Mrs K.R. Iremonger

92
93 G. Winfield
94 Rev M.L. Lesiter
95 Emma Burkinshaw
96 W.K. Newstead
97 Peter Charrett
98 Alan Taylor
99 R.A. Wheal
100 B.P. Holt
101 P. Cole
102 M.A. Smith
103 Philip Reeder
104 Miss Julie Wills
105 Mrs M. Hood
106 John Eames
107 Miss M. Kiff
108 Mrs A.L. Whitehouse
109 Barbara Le Brocq
110 Mrs N.P. Read
111 Stella Malhotra
112 W. Woods
113 Stuart Thorne
114 R.D.M. Gawn
115 Geoffrey Ries
116 Stuart Nagler
117 A.J.I. Jennings
118 H.R. Kirkwood
119 Ivy Hodder
120 N. Bruce Snyder
121 Joan Cowtan
122 C.M.W. Logan
123 Chris Ripper
124 John Vigor
125 Mrs W.A. Ottaway
126 J.M.G. Anthony
127 Giles Wright
128 Mr & Mrs K. Spalding
129 Dr D.A. Frye
130 Peter & Susan Upstone
131 G.J. Burrell
132 D.H. McKinley
133 Richard Timms
134 Mrs B.J. Smith
135 C.W. Thurston
136 Jacqui & Edward Solomons
137 J.V. Kisby
138 Derek Cole

139 John Burry
140 P.W. Kidd
141 Bernice & Anthony Conway
142 Rev Michael Carter
143 M.I. Cant
144 J. Conder
145 Ian M. Southern
146 Mrs J. Fletcher
147 G.T. Betts
148 Andrew Lawrence
149 R.G. Marshall
150 May S. Gregg
151 C.W. Maxwell
152 Brian Thurlow
153 Madeleine Carbonel
154 Dr & Mrs F. Whitham
155 Jacques G. Lay
156 Dr A. Lynn
157 Mrs C.N. Shadwell
158 John Pearson
159 D.J. Whiting
160 M.I. Sugar
161 Mrs K. Schon
162 Dr J.D. Gold
163 Mrs June Eager
164 Mrs B.R. Allen
165 W. Lampard
166 P.H. Halsey
167 Jonathan & Stella Marks
168 Allan N. Hertz
169 I. Osbourne
170 R.J. Halmshaw
171 Mrs M. Raettig
172 M.T. Anderson
173 Michael Gratton
174 B. Wing
175 P. Jenkins
176 Jan Keeley
177 Brian Barnard
178 David Freedman
179 Valerie Green
180 Stanton D. Smith
181 Jeanette & Andrew Lynch
182 Kenneth Gray
183 E.N.L. Pank

184 Pat Holland
185 Alison Sinclair
186 G.M. Lonsdale
187 P.R. & W. Draper
188 G. Marsh
189 Eve & Cyril Johnson
190 Peter Robert Beebee
191 N.B. Jakeman
192 Mr & Mrs R.J. Oakes-Monger
193 John N. Ratcliffe
194 Mr & Mrs W.R.H. Hakewell
195 P.A. Strong
196 Dr M.J. Bissett
197 E.C. Kirton
198 Mrs W.E. Padgett
199 Mrs J.P. Skilton
200 P.L. Anders
201
202 Mrs C. Davies
203 Sir Patrick Graham
204 Caroline Parsons
205 A.S. MacVine
206 Estelle Samuelson
207 Timothy J. Harris
208 C.D. Timpson
209 Alan M. Harris
210 Dr G.M. Fitzgerald
211 J.M. Kerslake Stead
212 Leslie A. Chappell
213 H.G. Beeton
214 Ronald G. Leaver
215
216 Sir Reginald Murley
217
218 Harold Walter Hill
219 Anthony Flynn
220
221 J.F. Lehain
222 E. Papalexis
223 Richard Guignard
224 David E. Havens
225 Mrs S.J. Dobson
226 S. Rosenbaum
227 D.G. Perks
228 Mr & Mrs S. Cohen
229 Jean M. Cooke
230 J. Bullman
231 Jennifer Day
232 Professor R.M.T. Hill
233 Richard Chalmers
234 John Mason
235 J.E. Parkin
236 Mrs C. McCabe
237 M.A. Fulford
238 R.A. Kenny
239 D.M. Thomas
240 L. Lambert
241 Peter Bowler
242 G.H. Bullwinkle
243 Keith Hughes
244 A. Rubin

245 Mr & Mrs R. Breward
246 B.C. Bennett
247 M.St C. Baird
248 Valerie Orsich
249 David J. Coombes
250 Edward Childs
251 Victor Davis
252 P.C. & F.A. Turner
253 Lilian F. Rogers
254 Mrs F. Carrington
255 Judith Cyprien
256 James & Amanda Kilsby
257 John Tattersall
258 Dr Peter Wigodsky
259 Howard Field
260 Michael Norton
261 Marina Dätwiler
262 Mrs J. Zetter
263 Alan & Susan Taub
264 Dr & Mrs R.N. Adams
265 Mr & Mrs P.D. Edwards
266 G.H. Brooks
267 D.G. Johnson
268 Mrs E.B. Gofton
269 Anthony Beal
270 F.D. Biddle
271 M.E. Drury
272 Derek & Ann Knight
273 W.G. Tilston-Jones
274 Eric Lobb
275 J.F. Tweddle
276 J.W. Bird
277 G.D. & J.M. Swaine
278 Charlotte R. Swaine
279 Katherine V. Swaine
280 Cllr Graham A. Nunn
281 Peter B. Clarke
282 Daphne J. Mercer
283 Robert Reith
284
285 Mrs P.B. Lilley
286 Joseph Sopher
287 J.M. Dennes
288 Mrs P. Brown
289 Dennis C. Smith
290 P.S. Vincent
291 Martin Delaney
292 Henry Connor
293 J.M. Reid
294 David K. Warby
295 H.C. Wood
296 A.P. Szymura
297 G. & D. Keen
298 Owen Ingram
299 C.D. Johnson
300 Philatelic Exporter Ltd
301 Mrs R. Waterman
302 M.J. Ablett
303 Mrs B. Brodie
304 B.G. Thomas
305 Dr J. Ripley

306
307 N. Friedlos
308 Alan Hedley
309 R.H. Wakely
310 T.F. Hart
311 Eileen M. Fraser
312 A.D. Sheridan
313 J.F. MacGregor
314 Robert Crowley
315 Dr James T. Farquhar
316 Brian Sobell
317 Eric J. Askew
318 R.A.B. Clough
319 Maisie Greaves
320 C. Culham
321 A.J.R. Vine
322 J. Park
323
324 M.L.J. Dexter
325 G.W. Kayley
326 Chris Babayode
327 Mrs J.C. Angel
328 Mrs L.J. Barton
329 G.E. Nosworthy
330 Mrs Jill Whitfield
331 H.M. Saunders
332 Shenley Village Society
333 D. Stafferton
334
335 Lord Aldenham
336 John Barnett
337 Sophie Strong
338 A.V. Warby
339 Mr & Mrs C. Gunner
340 Mrs B. Tubbs
341
342 T.J. Harris
343 Dennis Ross
344 Mr & Mrs G. Bell
345 D.H. Slaughter
346 David Robertson
347 Leonard Wright
348 Miss M. Gomm & Mrs M. Hearn
349 Mrs D. Woodcock
350 F.G. Lines
351 Mr & Mrs R.B. Jakeman
352 P.W. Burrell
353 Mary Hanson
354 Jack Lyon
355 P.T. Carrington
356 Douglas Brown
357 Cllr Peter Hand
358 Mrs Maisie Mitchell
359 Michael King
360 Margaret Rose
361 Stephen J. Hurst
362 Joyce Clapp
363 Roundbush Garage Ltd
364 Stuart Robinson
365 Beryl Walton

366 Mrs S.J. Newman
367 Denis J. Prior
368 Mrs S. Godding
369 Mr & Mrs I. Gray
370 Mrs Mary Wood
371 M. Pickford
372
373 M.C. Major
374 K.P. Edwards
375 Tom Haworth
376 Mrs Charlotte Phillips
377 Mrs Lynne Barnett
378 Giles Turner
379
380 C.G. Dexter
381 David Stephen George
382 Mrs E. Cornelissen
383 D. Stanley
384 Mrs P.R. Calder
385 John J. McGinley
386 Simon J. Masman
387 A.J. Mitchell
388
389 Hermione Lamb
390 D. Thornton
391 P.D. Wadey
392 S.R. Chybalski
393 Mrs R. Slade
394 Mrs G. Whitfield
395 Mr & Mrs Paul Howarth
396
397 A.L. Whitehouse
398 Mrs A.L. Ficker
399 Ron Richer
400
401 Mrs J. Barrett
402 Mrs A. Ficker
403 John E. Jennings
404 James P. Cruickshank
405 Wayne Bickerton
406
407 Howard Guard
408 B. Cook
409 Mrs R.E. Court
410 Mrs J.E. Shire
411 M. James Snyder
412 Mrs M.A. Melvin
413 Mrs E. Oakley
414 G. John Wilson
415 Miss Joan Cole CBE
416 Mrs J. Edney
417 Aleks Kotulski
418 N. Gerald
419 M.H. Pattinson
420 Kathleen Tungay
421 G.J. Burrell
422 Peter & Beryl Haxby
423 Ian M. Sher
424 Mrs Burrows
425
426 J. Giblin

Remaining names unlisted

ENDPAPERS — FRONT: The Aldenham Enclosure map of 1803, and
BACK: the 6in OS map in the first edition of 1871.